CARD SORTING
DESIGNING USABLE CATEGORIES

T0257661

Donna Spencer

Rosenfeld Media
Brooklyn, New York

Card Sorting: Designing Usable Categories
By Donna Spencer

Rosenfeld Media, LLC
705 Carroll Street, #2L
Brooklyn, New York
11215 USA

On the Web: www.rosenfeldmedia.com
Please send errors to: errata@rosenfeldmedia.com

Publisher: Louis Rosenfeld
Development Editor: David Womack
Editor/Production Editor: Marta Justak
Interior Layout Tech: Danielle Foster
Cover Design: The Heads of State
Indexer: Fred Leise
Proofreader: Heather Urschel

ISBN: 1-933820-02-0
ISBN: 978-1-933820-02-6
LCCN: 2009920137
Printed and bound in the United States of America

HOW TO USE THIS BOOK

At its core, card sorting is a pretty simple technique—write things on index cards (or the software equivalent) and ask people to sort the cards into groups.

But as is the case with most simple things, there is plenty of room for complexity. Figuring out why you would bother to do this in the first place; deciding what to put on the cards; guiding people through the activity so you get something useful; and actually applying what you've learned—all these can get pretty tricky for real-life messy projects.

That's why I wrote a whole book on card sorting—to share what I've learned via lots of card sorts and via working on projects where I had to organize information that people could easily find, understand, and use.

This is a practical book with a touch of theory and interesting real-life case studies. It is based on work that I, and many others, do day-to-day. I hope it helps you with your day-to-day work as well.

Who Should Read This Book?

This book is for anyone who needs to organize information that other people have to use. It will be particularly useful for people involved in information architecture projects (which I describe much better in Chapter 1).

If you have never run a card sort and are thinking of doing so, this book is definitely for you. By the end, you'll be able to plan your sort, run it, and figure out what you've learned.

If you've run card sorts already, this book is for you, too. I've included plenty of tips based on my experience, and you may really like the chapters on analysis (9 and 10), especially if you have never attempted statistical analysis in the past.

And if you don't think you'll ever run a card sort, but have a team that might need to do so, there's plenty of valuable information here for you. You'll be able to better support your team when they ask if they can run a sort (or do other user research). You may get the most from Chapters 1 and 2, and how the outcomes of card sorting are used for projects.

What's in This Book?

This book is organized into four main sections.

Chapters 1 and 2 provide **background**. Chapter 1 covers what card sorting is all about, why you'd do it, and how it fits in a project. Chapter 2 is not about card sorting at all, but is instead about some of the really important principles that underlie categorization and why it is hard to organize things.

Chapters 3 through 8 cover all the **practical steps to run a card sort**, including choosing your method, selecting cards, arranging participants, making cards, and facilitating the session. This whole section is very practical and full of tips and tricks.

Chapters 9 and 10 are all about **analysis**—extracting insights from the card sort data and observations. Chapter 9 is about exploratory analysis and Chapter 10 is about statistical analysis (that's the scariest chapter).

The last section is about **using what you have learned**. Chapter 11 teaches you how to apply the outcomes to your projects, and in Chapter 12 you'll learn about communicating the results.

What Comes with the Book?

This book's companion website (♏ rosenfeldmedia.com/books/ cardsorting/) contains pointers to useful card-sorting resources, such as my card sort analysis spreadsheet, a list of card-sorting tools, and a card-sorting bibliography, as well as a calendar of my upcoming talks and a place for you to engage in discussion with others who are interested in card sorting. You can keep up with the site by subscribing to its RSS feed (♏ feeds.rosenfeldmedia.com/cardsorting/).

We've also made the book's diagrams, screenshots, and other illustrations available under a Creative Commons license for you to download and include in your own presentations. You'll find the original illustrations and diagrams from this book at www.flickr.com/photos/rosenfeldmedia.

FREQUENTLY ASKED QUESTIONS

I wrote our content on cards/sticky notes and our team shuffled it around to create the IA. That's a card sort, isn't it?

Not really. That's just shuffling content ideas around the table (which is still useful, just not really a card sort). I think the essential element to something being a card sort is that it involves real users of your information. See Chapter 1 for more information on what a card sort involves.

I need to test that my draft information architecture is okay. Should I do a closed card sort?

A closed card sort is where you ask people to slot content into a set of categories that you give them. It is useful to learn about where they think content goes, but a closed card sort will not tell you whether they will be able to find it. If you need to make sure that people can find information in your IA, you should give them a set of tasks and ask where they would look. See page 149 for more information on how to test your information architecture.

My website is really big. How do I get the card sort to cover it all?

This can be really tricky because you can't just give people an enormous pile of cards. You can sort with topics instead of detailed content, focus on just part of the site at a time, or run a series of sorts to get good coverage. More tips for large sites are on page 70.

How many people should I involve so the answer is statistically significant?

Statistical significance is really not important—you want insights and ideas rather than the one true answer. You should involve enough people so that you see enough similarities and differences to help with your design project. More tips on selecting people are in Chapter 6.

Should I let people put cards in more than one place?

Participants often ask if they can put cards in more than one place, especially when there is not one clear home for a card. I always allow them to do so. It gives me useful information about content that may cross categories. See page 99 for more questions participants ask.

What do I do with all this data?

Ah, that is the big question. Spend some time just looking for patterns and "interesting" things in the data. Then dig a bit deeper and look at similarities and differences. You may not get one perfect answer, but you'll always learn interesting things for your project. Read about analysis in Chapters 9 and 10.

I don't remember my university statistics. How do I analyze all this?

If you don't know how to do statistics, that's okay. Don't try! There are ways to analyze data without statistics—exploring it, looking for patterns, identifying similarities and differences. And you'll learn more than if you plugged it into a statistics tool and got an answer. But make sure you don't collect more information than you need, or this will be impossible to do. See Chapters 9 and 10 for information on how to analyze with and without statistics.

TABLE OF CONTENTS

CHAPTER 3
Defining the Need 43

CHAPTER 4
Choose the Method 51

CHAPTER 5
Choose the Content 61

CHAPTER 6
Choose the People 73

CHAPTER 11
Use What You've Learned

APPENDIX
Documentation

FOREWORD

There's something about cards. Cards can turn the drab and mundane into something strangely exciting. Recipe cards, for example, have a peculiar allure that cookbooks lack. A book full of tables of baseball statistics? Dull as dishwater. Put those same stats on the backs of trading cards, however, and now you've got something.

You'll see this same pattern unfold whenever card sorting is included in a user research session. Maybe the research participants have already been asked to poke at a prototype design, or they've simply answered a bunch of questions about their attitudes and preferences. In any case, their demeanor inevitably changes when the cards come out for sorting. "What's this?" they seem to be saying to themselves. "This doesn't look like what I expected. This looks like it might actually be...fun!"

I don't think this reaction can be attributed to their enthusiasm for the task they're being presented with. There are a hundred ways you could ask someone to help you organize content for a website, but the 99 ways to accomplish this goal that don't involve cards aren't likely to provoke the same interested response.

Perhaps it's because cards don't seem like a serious tool to people. After all, for most of us, our first encounter with cards as children was not as something people did work with—it was as something people played with. And a stack of cards truly is an invitation to play: to hold them in our hands, to shuffle, deal, flip, match, stack, and sort.

That's not all there is to it, of course. There is some deep satisfaction to be derived from simply finding a place for everything and putting it there, which surely explains part of the appeal for card sorting—and, indeed, the entire practice of information architecture. Like all the good card games we played as children (and many of us still play today), card sorting is about the tension between randomness and order, a tension the human mind finds infinitely engaging.

Exploring that tension is itself a kind of play. In this book, Donna Spencer lays out the rules of the game. Knowing those rules will help you get the most out of this deceptively simple technique. People often miss the subtleties involved in using card sorting effectively, but with Spencer as your guide, you can be sure of the best way to play your cards.

— Jesse James Garrett,
   author of *The Elements of User Experience* and president, Adaptive Path

All About Card Sorting

An entire book on card sorting? *Card sorting?*
Well, it's about more than just rearranging note-cards into navigation.

When I started writing this book, I decided to ask friends and family to do a card sort based on supermarket groceries. I thought this would be a fairly straightforward exercise and hoped to get a neat, consistent outcome that I could use to illustrate ideas for the book. I should have known better.

I wrote the names of grocery items on note-cards and asked the participants to organize them into categories that made the most sense to them. It turned out that everyone organized the groceries differently. Some people created groups according to how a supermarket is usually organized (canned food, snack food), some by cuisine (Mexican, Thai, Indian), and some by cooking method (baking, grilling, microwave). My eight-year-old daughter organized the cards according to taste and texture, making groups for runny things (soup, tinned fruit), things with flour (bread, biscuits), sweet things (chocolate, cookies, sugar), and unsweet things.

As this example demonstrates, how people organize items can be idiosyncratic and highly personal.

The purpose of this book is to enable you to use card sorting to explore the different ways that items can be categorized and determine what organizational method works best for your project. Card sorting can be particularly useful in situations in which you need to come up with a new organizational scheme but don't know where to start; when you know that the current organizational scheme isn't working but aren't sure why; or when you want to test whether one particular organizational scheme is more intuitive than another.

Card sorting is simple, fun, and cheap. I've used it on loads of projects, tried different ways of doing it, and thought about what works and doesn't. And now I've written it all down. Yes, in a book.

My First Card Sort

How did I find my way to card sorting?

I was designing the information architecture for a large government website. The navigation categories had evolved over time and weren't labeled clearly, so people had a lot of trouble finding even basic information. I now recognize this as a common problem, but at the time I just felt overwhelmed. The fact that this was a government site, and so contained essential information, added pressure—if potential users couldn't find the information they needed, it would be my fault.

I had been tasked with reorganizing and relabeling the main groups of content on the home page and second-level pages. I had some ideas for how the content could be organized, based mainly on my own intuition. But how could I be sure that the categories that made sense to me would also make sense to someone else?

What's more, the team I was working with had been developing the website from the beginning. They weren't about to restructure it just because the new kid thought something made sense—they wanted "evidence" that my intuitions were correct. Whatever I came up with, I'd have to be able to back it up.

I had a rough understanding of card sorting: write content ideas on index cards and ask people to make groups out of them. I'd heard that this, somehow, could help me figure out how to organize the content. It wasn't much to go on, but given the situation, it sounded at least worth a try.

I got some index cards from the office supply, wrote the content title on the front, and printed and glued a couple of paragraphs of the content on the back. I then invited internal staff and some external users to participate in the experiment.

While they worked in groups of three, I watched and listened to the conversations. To my surprise, the experiment went smoothly—everyone found it easy, fun, and it didn't even take much time.

By the end, the participants had created a number of consistent groups with similar cards in them, and the places where there were differences gave me a better understanding of how they thought about particular content items. Finally, I had some research to back up my recommendation.

Not only did the team agree to give my new organizational scheme a try, but also the new IA actually worked! Although seven years have passed and the website has been expanded and redesigned a couple of times, the categories from that card sort are still in use and still seem to be working well.

What Is Card Sorting?

Card sorting is best understood not as a collaborative method for creating navigation, but rather as a tool that helps us understand the people we are designing for.

The method is fairly straightforward. You give people a set of cards (often paper index cards) that have example content written on them. You ask people to sort the cards into piles according to what's similar and describe the groups they make (this is called an *open card sort*, as illustrated in Figure 1.1). Or you can give people a set of content cards plus a set of categories and ask them to sort the cards into the predetermined categories (this is called a *closed card sort*, as illustrated in Figure 1.2). Either way, you record the results, analyze them, and apply what you learned to your project.

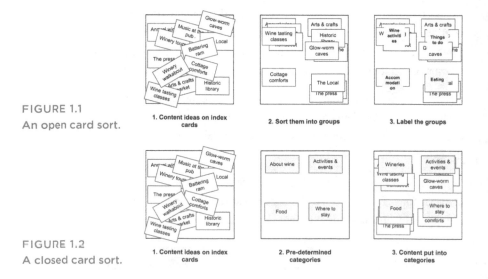

FIGURE 1.1
An open card sort.

FIGURE 1.2
A closed card sort.

Although it sounds simple, card sorting can be a very powerful technique. You learn a lot about how people think about categories and concepts, how they describe them, and what information belongs to a category. This is incredibly useful when you want to organize information in a way so that other people can find it.

Steps in a Card Sort

The main steps in a card sort are as follows:

1. Decide what you want to learn.

2. Select the method (open or closed, face-to-face or remote, manual or software).

3. Choose content.

4. Choose and invite participants.

5. Run the card sort and record the data (see Figure 1.3).

6. Analyze the outcomes (see Figure 1.4).

7. Use them in your project (see Figure 1.5).

FIGURE 1.3
Sort the cards.

FIGURE 1.4
Analyze the results.

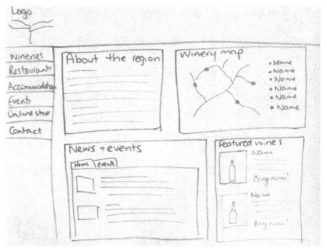

FIGURE 1.5
Use what you learn
to design categories.

How Card Sorting Is Used

Although card sorting has a long history in social research (where it is
known as sorting, pile sorting, free sorting, and free grouping), these days
the most common use of card sorting is for information architecture (IA)
projects. An IA project is one where the focus is on organizing, grouping,

and labeling items (often content) that other people use. Common types of IA projects include:

- Planning the structure and navigation for website or intranet design projects

- Structuring online help

- Creating a classification scheme for a document-management system

- Identifying potential categories for a knowledge-base

- Determining menu groups and subgroups for a software application

- Identifying key steps and substeps in a process

- Figuring out the structure of a book (no, I didn't card sort my book, but I was tempted)

Card sorting can be used in many ways in information architecture projects. Common uses include:

- Brainstorming different categorization models

- Exploring how people think about a certain topic

- Finding out what categories seem similar or complementary

- Learning about what goes together and what doesn't

- Gathering lists of words people use to describe groups of information

Users are always full of surprises. They never fail to perceive connections that we (the project team) never anticipated. Sometimes this has turned our anticipated organization on its head and led to a better one. Most useful of all, however, is the peek inside users' mental models of site content.

—Dave Rogers

This list alone provides reason enough to consider card sorting when organizing a large amount of information. But card sorting is useful in other ways as well.

By providing insight into how other people might organize information, card sorting may lead you to question your assumptions. If you're working on the redesign of a big website and already know the content very well, it can be hard to get a fresh perspective and come up with new organizational schemes. A card sort can help you see the content from the perspective of someone coming to it for the first time.

Card sorting can also help teams come to a consensus. Imagine that you're part of a team designing a big website from scratch. Some team members think the website should be organized one way, and others think it should be done a different way. You actually don't know which will be best. By providing an external perspective, card sorting can help you decide which organizational scheme is likely to be useful for most people, most of the time.

> *The most effective use of card sorting is in its social benefits. Even where I might not find card sorting "effective," I might use it just as an excuse for an engaging activity where a group of people need to learn to work together and focus on the details of a universe of information.*
>
> —Paula Thornton

A Word of Caution

Card sorting has come under criticism from practitioners who find the technique doesn't give them the results they expected, and from social researchers who think practitioners are being sloppy in their application of the technique. These criticisms are often justified. Although I believe card sorting can be a rich source of insights, it should be used in combination with other techniques, as well as with common sense. I have seen projects where the outcomes from a card sort were simply picked up and used as navigation with little or no analysis or verification.

As with any other tool or technique, it's important to use card sorting for the right reasons, at the right time in the project, and to analyze the results in combination with other inputs.

Complementary User Research Techniques

Card sorting is one of a family of user research techniques designed to give you insight into how people think.

But why would you care how people think anyway? No reason—unless you want other people to use what you're designing. It's all too easy to assume that other people think about things the same way you do. But if you don't test this assumption, you're likely to end up with a result that other people don't like, don't understand, and can't use. I bet you can think of plenty of products and websites like that.

Case Study: Blinded by Science

A couple of years back, I was working with a team to redesign their intranet. The intranet was organized according to the business structure (as intranets often are), and staff couldn't find anything. They needed to know who did what before knowing where to look, and the company was so big that no one knew who did what.

But the managers couldn't understand what the problem was. That was our first challenge—showing management that the staff didn't think in the same way as they did.

Our second challenge was that this was a company full of scientists. Being scientists, they wouldn't believe anything unless we could clearly illustrate how we came up with it. The team had tried to reorganize the content themselves before and just weren't able to get changes accepted.

Card sorting was a natural fit for this project. We would use it to show how the staff thought the intranet content should fit together, and clearly show how we came up with our structure. And, of course, we could get good information to support the ideas we already had for how to organize the content.

We didn't use card sorting alone—we also interviewed staff and spent a lot of time understanding the content. But the card sort was one of the key inputs to the structure, and definitely key to showing transparency and demonstrating our process.

Although I'm a fan of card sorting (obviously), I would never suggest it is the only technique you should use in a project. Even though it is particularly good at helping you learn about how people think about groupings in content, it doesn't help you to learn about what people need or how they undertake tasks.

On any project where I run a card sort, I always conduct other user research as well. The three approaches I use most often[1] and how they fit with card sorting are outlined in the following sections.

Interviews

Interviews are one of my favorite user research techniques (probably because I like talking with people). An interview is a discussion with a person or a very small group, often in the normal setting of work or home, about issues relating to a project. An interview may also include some time where you simply observe the interviewees going about their normal tasks.

Interviews are excellent for gathering rich, targeted information about the issues affecting your project, including the context in which people work, their tasks, their skills, and their information needs. Interviews can be very flexible, letting you explore issues and tangents as they are discussed. If an interview is conducted in the workplace or home, people can show you how they work and provide concrete examples of the issues you are discussing.

The main disadvantage of interviews is that they can be time-consuming, both to organize and to run.

An interview can be a great way of following up on insights you gain during the card sort. And both interviews and card sorts provide information on how people describe content.

---

1 These are just my favorites—there are many other methods. To learn more about these and others, I recommend *Observing the User Experience: A practitioner's guide to user research*, by Mike Kuniavsky (2003, Morgan Kaufmann).

Surveys

I also like using surveys in information architecture projects. In a survey, people are provided with a set of questions and asked to fill in answers. Surveys can be done on paper or online. They can be *quantitative* (with closed questions that can then be statistically analyzed), *qualitative* (with open text-based questions), or a *combination* of both. You can collect information about how people use a website, what they may need in the future, and many other issues of interest.

Surveys are particularly good for gathering a large number of responses with less effort than individual interviews. I always allow plenty of free-text responses in surveys to encourage people to provide detail with their answers.

Although data from surveys tends to be less in-depth than other methods— it is rarely possible to follow up with each participant—surveys allow you to easily compare and contrast the responses of large numbers of individuals, providing a rich source of data.

If you are running a survey online, you could ask people to complete online card sorts immediately after they finish the survey. Indeed, some card sorting software includes the capability to include survey questions.

Analysis of Existing Information

You can often gain a wealth of information by looking at existing interactions. This is particularly true online, where user-tracking software is increasingly common.

- Website statistics provide data about content people are already using, the areas of the site that are most popular, and content that is rarely visited.

- Search terms (from an internal search facility and external search sites) provide an insight into key information needs and how people describe things.

- Customer emails, letters, forums, call-center logs, and help-desk queries can tell you how people talk about a certain need or feature.

All these sources provide great information about the language people use to describe what they are interested in. I've even used search terms as the content for a card sort.

Good Company

I'm not the only one who combines card sorting with other techniques. I recently asked information architecture and usability folks what complementary techniques they used on the most recent project in which they used card sorting.

Interviews	70%
Existing sources of user data, such as website statistics and search logs	66%
Usability tests	53%
Task analysis	46%
Surveys or questionnaires	42%
Focus groups	6%

Timing of Card Sorts in a Project

I once mistimed a card sorting activity. Through a strange set of events, I inherited a project schedule from someone else. (I also inherited a project manager obsessed with following "the plan.") The project schedule had a usability test and card sort as the first two activities in a project. I think the original idea was to get feedback on what was wrong with the current website and get ideas for improvements in one step. I had little time to prepare, so, as a shortcut, I used the website's site map for card content. During the activity, each participant did the usability test and then the card sort.

It was a failure in many ways. Participants' results from the card sort were influenced by the current website structure, so we didn't get much value from their groupings. I later found out that the site map hadn't been updated for a while, but the content had been updated, so the cards didn't reflect the actual content. I didn't know enough about the domain to ask the right questions of the participants while I had the chance. In the end, the card sort was a complete waste of time.

But when I can write my own project schedule (which is most of the time), I prefer to run a card sort after I have learned something about the project, the users, and the content. At this time in a project, I know what questions I want to explore and know enough to plan the card sort so I get the most out of it.

I prefer to use a card sort early in the project because it helps me explore broader questions about content groups and may raise questions I can follow up on during the project. Later in a project, card sorting can be used to explore more specific questions—for example, you may want to focus on a smaller section of the content or gather additional labeling ideas.

> *I've found that clients tend to expect a black-and-white outcome from card sorting—to see answers rather than more questions. Sometimes the reason to do a card sort is to work out what questions we need to ask, or where we really need to concentrate our efforts.*
>
> —Leisa Reichelt (disambiguity.com)

The key prerequisite for a card sort is that you understand the content you'll be working with—otherwise, you won't be able to choose suitable content or ask good questions.

Sometimes you will choose not to run a card sort at all. Although useful, it isn't a mandatory project activity. Don't run a card sort if you already have enough research and a good understanding of the categorization you want to use.

Let's Get Sorting

Now that you know what card sorting is all about, you may be ready to start your project. In the next chapter, I'll take a short tangent to explain some basic concepts of information architecture—why it is hard to organize things, and some structure, classification, and categorization principles. Then in Chapters 3–7, I'll get into the practical preparation steps— choosing how to run the activity, figuring out who to involve, choosing content, and preparing cards.

Chapter 1 Summary/Tips

There are two types of card sorting:

- Open: You give cards with content ideas to people to group however it makes sense to them.

- Closed: You give people cards, and also a set of predetermined categories to put the cards into.

Card sorting can help you:

- See different ways information could be grouped.

- Learn how users perceive groups of content.

- Learn about how people think about a topic.

- Find out what goes together and what doesn't.

- Gather lists of words people use to describe groups of information.

Card sorting is just one of many complementary user research techniques.

CHAPTER 2

All About Organizing

This is the theory chapter. Don't let that scare you. Why do I have a chapter on theory in what is otherwise a very practical book? Well, I figure that no one (except me) runs a card sort just for the fun of it. After all, your real goal isn't to run a card sort—it's to organize content so it makes sense to the people who will use it. And if the ultimate goal is to organize things, it is awfully handy to understand some fundamental principles of organization and classification. I promise that when you start applying card sorting to your project, you'll find this information useful.

Of course, if you already know about organization and classification, feel free to skip this chapter entirely. And if you are keen to get into the practical planning steps, jump to the next chapter and come back to this one later.

The Challenges of Organizing

One of the main reasons for doing a card sort is to learn how other people think of groups, concepts, and categories. Since this is something people have been doing for several million years, it's not surprising that some patterns have emerged. We'll spend most of this chapter looking at those patterns. First, though, let's take a look at some of the reasons why organization continues to challenge us.

More Than One Approach

I have an ongoing problem with my wine rack. There are too many ways to organize it. At the moment, my wine is grouped first by color (white at the top, red at the bottom) and then by varietal (Riesling, sauvignon blanc, chardonnay, and so on). Within the varietal, the wines are arranged by vintage (oldest to youngest). I stick a label on the end showing when I got it and when to drink it by, as you can see in Figure 2.1. I keep being tempted to rethink my wine rack. I could organize it by winery, when to drink it, or I could separate out the wine to drink with a special meal from the drink-everyday wine. Luckily, I have other things to do.

FIGURE 2.1
Part of my wine rack—white wines on top, reds on bottom, and varietals on each shelf, with a label on the end of each bottle.

Most types of information lend themselves to different methods of organization. Recipes, for example, can be organized by dish, ingredient, cuisine, or celebrity chef. Clothes can be organized by garment type, season, or color. A corporate intranet can be organized by topic, team, or date updated.

The digital world presents unique challenges and opportunities. Physical items can be arranged only one way at a time—they just can't exist in two places. In the digital world, we can use more than one organization method or duplicate a resource. For example, I could create a digital version of my wine rack and organize it in a hundred different ways.

Everyone Thinks Differently

When I teach information architecture, I always ask my students how they organize their bookshelves. Most people do it in a fairly predictable way—by subject, genre, or author. But some organize according to size, the Dewey decimal system, and even color. (Of course, there are people like me who have so many books they are just in random piles. Do you think I can get away with saying they are organized spatially?)

But can you imagine trying to find a particular book in someone else's bookshelf if they have organized their books by size or color? What if you'd never actually seen the book before? And the Dewey decimal system definitely wouldn't work for me—I haven't a clue about the numbers and most of my books would be in just one or two categories.

Context Matters

When my garden is overflowing with apples, tomatoes, and peppers, I want to find as many recipes that include those ingredients as possible. But, more often, I want something less specific—for example, if I've decided to make a Thai duck curry, I may want to find an interesting starter to go with it or an appropriate Thai dessert. These different contexts suggest different organizational methods for the content—luckily, I have one cookbook organized by main ingredient, and many others that cover different cuisines arranged by course.

Context also matters for website content. The Information Architecture Summit (see iasummit.org/) is an annual conference about, as you may guess, information architecture. At different times of the year, people do different tasks with the website. Early in the year, they need to find dates and conference topics, so the focus is on broad, general information. Later, they'll need to decide whether they can attend, so they'll need to know costs and details of individual sessions. When they arrive at the conference, they'll need to find out where dinners and parties are. I've managed the website in the past and changed the structure during the year to accommodate these different tasks, as shown in Figures 2.2 and 2.3.

IA Summit 2008

(v1.0 - draft wireframes...)

Home

About the IA Summit

News

Call for proposals

Previous conferences

IA Summit 2008

The Information Architecture Summit is the premier gathering place for those interested in information architecture. The 2007 IA Summit attracted over 570 attendees, including beginners, experienced IAs, and people from a range of related fields. Read more about the summit and what people have said about it.

Call for Proposals

The call for regular presentations, panels, management track, posters and pre-conference sessions has now closed. We had a great response - 140 regular presentations, 12 panels, 13 management track, 25 posters and a whopping 39 pre-conference session proposals.

We're now in the blind peer review stage - where for the next 3 weeks about 50 volunteer will write close to 1000 reviews in the unenviable task of trying to pick about 50 sessions from 165 proposals!

2008 Theme: Experiencing Information

The 2008 theme of "Experiencing Information" shifts the focus back to users. A user experience exists only to allow people to "do things" (in the broadest sense ... buying books, sharing photos with friends, looking

Conference details

IA Summit 2008: "Experiencing Information"

April 10-14, 2008

Hyatt Regency, Miami, Florida, USA

News

Death by Powerpoint

September 30. 2007

We're about half-way through the submission period and some really interesting entries are coming in. As I was looking through them I started thinking about some of the really great ideas I've heard that have been compromised by a poor...

Continue reading "Death by Powerpoint" »

The 2008 IA Summit Venue - comments & photos

August 31. 2007

Since we received so many comments about

FIGURE 2.2

The IA Summit website early in the year—focusing on broad information and the call for proposals.

The Information Architecture Summit is the premier gathering place for information architects. Everyone who touches on IA is welcome to share and learn.

Last year the summit attracted 560 attendees, from beginners to those considered the top experts in the field. (see what they said about it)

Registration is open

Early bird pricing ends February 22nd!Register now.

Crowdvine network

Our social networking app. Crowdvine

FIGURE 2.3

The IA Summit website closer to the conference—focusing on registration and the program.

Words Are Tricky

Organizing requires labeling—describing groups, categories, and items. Any group of items can be described in many ways. There may be colloquial phrases, regional terms, internal jargon, synonyms, and so on.

Choosing the right label for a concept can be tricky. If there are only a few people using the information, you can call an item anything you like (as long as everyone remembers what you mean). For example, when your Mom asks for the "whatsit," your Dad knows to hand her the remote control. But much of our work organizing information relies on good labels and descriptions that are generally well understood. Think of how many terms exist for the most basic of interactions: click, select, hit, choose, or point your cursor at a link. Which term is best? And how about the "one of these things is not like the others" quandary? What exactly should you do when one of a group of terms—let's say headings for a menu—doesn't fit well with the others?

How Does Card Sorting Relate to Organizational Challenges?

Card sorting can help you learn what classification schemes exist for a set of information, whether people think in similar ways, and how context changes the way they describe groups. It won't tell you which term is best, but it might help you get a sense of how—and when—different terms are used, and which are most common. And card sorting won't tell you whether you should change that one strange term that employs a different tone or is jargony so that it matches the rest. But it will help you detect patterns, and ultimately, you'll be able to make a better decision about what do to.

All of this, of course, is useful when you need to organize information.

Structure: Hierarchies and Databases

How you structure your content determines the kinds of information you look for in a card sort. You may plan your card sort differently, depending on the structure of the final result.

Hierarchical Structure

A hierarchical structure, illustrated in Figure 2.4, is one where a group is broken up into subgroups, sub-subgroups, and so on. Or, looking at it from the bottom up, a set of objects is assembled into groups, broader groups, and even broader groups. The file system on your computer is a perfect example of a hierarchy—folders have subfolders and sub-subfolders, often many levels deep. An organization chart is another common example. The navigation of many websites also functions this way.

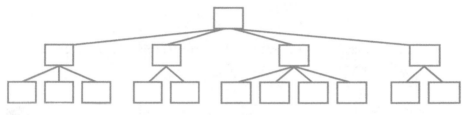

FIGURE 2.4
A hierarchy.

Hierarchical structures are very natural for humans to use and easy for people to understand—humans have always created informal hierarchies and have been creating formal hierarchies (often called taxonomies) for tens of thousands of years.[1]

Database Structure

Compared to a hierarchy, a database structure is completely flat—it is much more like a bucket of objects than a nested set of groups. Database structures are well suited to content that has a set of similar features, such as product catalogues, movies, or weblog posts.

In a database structure, each item is stored independently and described by a set of metadata. The metadata is then used to determine what will be displayed on a web page.

---

[1] Alex Wright's book *Glut: Mastering Information Through the Ages* (2007, Joseph Henry Press) provides an in-depth examination of human history as it relates to information and classification.

An example from the Information Architecture Summit will help to illustrate how database structures work. The conference presentations are stored in a database, and each has the following metadata:

- Title

- Speaker

- Abstract

- Start time and date

- Location

These fields can be used to display the presentations in a range of ways, as illustrated in Figures 2.5 and 2.6.

Sunday 25 March			
	Virginia II	Mesquite	Laughlin II
9:00 – 9:45 am	WebPatterns: design patterns in web site architecture and User Interaction - John Allsopp	Mobile information architecture: designing experiences for the mobile web - Christian Crumlish	My grandmother the information architect: The IA of everyday life - Hallie Wilfert
9:45	Morning tea		
10:15 – 11:00 am	How the advertising industry thinks - Eric Reiss	Rich mapping and soft systems: new tools for creating conceptual models - Gene Smith, Matthew Milan	Communicating design: an astonishingly close look at what makes IA documentation work - Dan Brown
11:00	Break		
11:15 – 12:15 pm	Where does IA fit in the design process? - Peter Boersma, Larisa Warnke, Peter Merholz, Livia Labate, Leisa	Real information architecture – new mighty deeds - Margaret Hanley, Lisa Chan, Tom Coates, Matt Biddulph	IA in Second Life - Stacy Merrill Surla, Lori Bell, Andrew Hinton, Beth Kanter, Peter Allison, Josh Knauer

FIGURE 2.5
Presentations can be organized by time and location in a schedule.

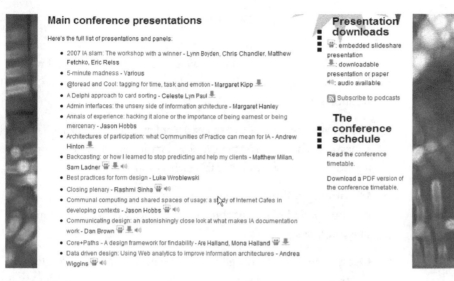

Main conference presentations

Here's the full list of presentations and panels:

- 2007 IA slam: The workshop with a winner - Lynn Boyden, Chris Chandler, Matthew Fetchko, Eric Reiss
- 5-minute madness - Various
- @toread and Cool: tagging for time, task and emotion - Margaret Kipp
- A Delphi approach to card sorting - Celeste Lyn Paul
- Admin interfaces: the unsexy side of information architecture - Margaret Hanley
- Annals of experience: hacking it alone or the importance of being earnest or being mercenary - Jason Hobbs
- Architectures of participation: what Communities of Practice can mean for IA - Andrew Hinton
- Backcasting: or how I learned to stop predicting and help my clients - Matthew Milan, Sam Ladner
- Best practices for form design - Luke Wroblewski
- Closing plenary - Rashmi Sinha
- Communal computing and shared spaces of usage: a study of Internet Cafes in developing contexts - Jason Hobbs
- Communicating design: an astonishingly close look at what makes IA documentation work - Dan Brown
- Core+Paths - A design framework for findability - Are Halland, Mona Halland
- Data driven design: Using Web analytics to improve information architectures - Andrea Wiggins

Presentation downloads

- : embedded slideshare presentation
- : downloadable presentation or paper
- : audio available

Subscribe to podcasts

The conference schedule

Read the conference timetable.

Download a PDF version of the conference timetable.

FIGURE 2.6
Or as an A-Z list by title.

How Does Card Sorting Relate to Structure?

Card sorting is a great method to help you create a hierarchical structure. By getting people to create groups and subgroups from bundles of cards, you are asking them to create a mini-hierarchy one level deep. You could ask your participants to expand the hierarchy during the card sort—creating additional groupings. Generally, however, I ask participants to focus on the main groups and then apply other research methods for fleshing out the hierarchy.

When you are working with a database structure, your approach would be slightly different. Rather than looking for the main content groupings, as you would when creating a hierarchy, card sorting can help you determine metadata for each content item. For the IA Summit website example, for instance, I could ask people to group the presentations by audience first, then by group, and then again by topic. I could use the outcomes to assign an audience and topic in each presentation's metadata. We could then allow users to find all presentations suitable for beginners, or all presentations on a particular topic.

Classification Schemes

As I mentioned, content can be organized many different ways—my wine can be organized by varietal, vintage, winery, price, or with whom I want to drink it. This slightly contrived example represents many different classification schemes:

- **Topic:** Wine varieties are organized according to a topic scheme. The wine topic scheme can be thought of as a small hierarchy—at the top level are red and white wines and within each are different grape varieties.

- **Chronology:** Vintage (the year the grapes were harvested) and drinking period represent chronological schemes—a point in time or a range of times.

- **Geography:** Region is a geographical scheme, representing a defined location where the wine is made.

- **Alphabetical order:** I could display a list of wineries in name order, using an alphabetic scheme.

- **Numerical order:** Price and age are both numeric schemes.

- **Task:** If I had wine to give away and to keep for myself, I could consider that a task scheme.

- **Audience:** I have wines that I drink with family, and those I drink with special friends. It's a stretch, but this could be considered an audience scheme.

These schemes aren't the definitive list. Some could be collapsed, for example. You could argue that alphabetical and numerical schemes are really flavors of a single *ordered* scheme. Conversely, some could be split—topics, for example, could include many ways to describe content—and many could overlap. Classification is ultimately an imperfect and messy undertaking; don't let yourself get caught up in the false goal of getting it "right."

Some content is naturally suited to a particular classification scheme, making the choice straightforward. Some content can be organized according to more than one classification scheme and you need to make a choice about which scheme (or schemes) you will use.

Topic

Topical classification schemes are very common—we use them more often than any other type of scheme. A topical classification scheme can be created for any set of content or objects, and can include many possible aspects of a given object. For example, wines may be classified topically by their *color, flavor, aroma*, and what kinds of *companion foods* they go with best.

Sometimes, you will use an existing topical scheme—such as an existing medical, library, botanical, or product classification. Often, you will create your own topical scheme that suits your content and users (see Figure 2.7).

FIGURE 2.7
Best Cellars breaks the traditional region-based model for wine and uses a topic scheme based on taste.

Chronology

A chronological scheme is well suited to content:

- That has a defined time or timeframe

- Where time is a key attribute of the content

- Where you know people would like to access the content according to the time period

Something to keep in mind with chronological schemes is that they don't suit all types of tasks. Although it is appropriate to display news according to the date it occurred, sports fans may also want to see the news about their favorite sport in one place (a sports topical scheme). If you are organizing events by time, you may also organize them according to location so people can see nearby events, or by topic so they can see all the baseball games, for example. Figure 2.8 shows an example.

FIGURE 2.8
Upcoming.org shows my events by date, but can also display them according to location and topic.

Geography

Geographical schemes are perfectly suited to anything that is location-based, such as travel and events.

Before using a geographical scheme, make sure that your users are going to want to access the information according to geography. For example, it would *not* be helpful to arrange a wine retail site solely by geography if you knew that most people wanted to find a cheap red wine to go with dinner and didn't mind where it came from. But it might be appropriate to arrange a wine tourism site by region so people could explore wineries in a defined area, as shown in Figure 2.9.

FIGURE 2.9
The Pure Tasmania website is arranged according to three distinctly different regions.

Alphabetical Order

Anything that can be given a name can be organized alphabetically by its name. An alphabetical scheme is most suitable when people:

- Know what they are looking for

- Know what to call it

- What they call it matches the way you label it

Alphabetical schemes are commonly used as a secondary organization method, when the main method may be one of the other schemes such as topic. Many websites and intranets, for example, use A-Z indexes (as do books, of course) or A-Z listings of articles (see Figure 2.10).

Alphabetical schemes do not suit all user tasks. When people have an idea of what they are looking for, but do not know what to call it, alphabetical schemes can be very hard to use.

FIGURE 2.10
BBC food has a great glossary organized alphabetically by name.

Numerical Order

A numerical scheme is well suited to content that can be counted or measured, and when users want to find information by number.

Numbers are more often used to sequence lists than to group content. For example, numbers can be used to sequence products by price, rainwater tanks by capacity, content pages by popularity, or sports results by performance (see Figure 2.11).

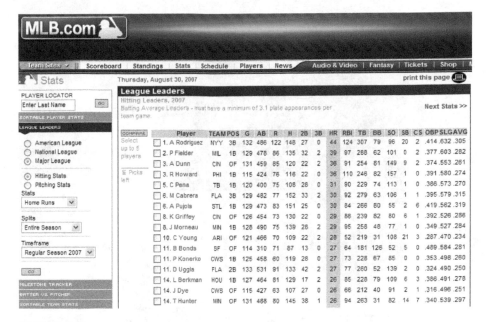

FIGURE 2.11
Baseball statistics are sequenced by performance.

Task

Task schemes are best suited to situations where people need to complete a set of clearly differentiated tasks and you can easily map content or actions to the tasks.

Task schemes are more common in applications (where people must complete a series of steps) than in content-rich websites (where the main task is to find information). See Figure 2.12.

FIGURE 2.12
Wine.com uses a task scheme for the main entry point to the website (shop, send, learn).

Audience

Audience schemes are most suitable when:

- You can clearly identify your audiences.

- People can easily associate with one of these audiences.

- Your content is clearly addressed toward a particular audience.

Achieving all three criteria can be tricky. I have worked on intranet projects where the design team wanted to group the content according to audience—managers, administrative, support, and sales staff. When we tried to allocate content to each group, we found that most content was relevant to at least two groups (often all four). When we talked to sales managers, they weren't sure whether they should use the manager's section or the sales section. We opted for a topic scheme instead (see Figure 2.13).

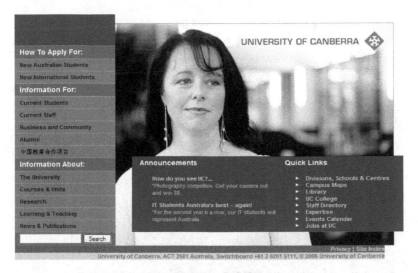

FIGURE 2.13
The University of Canberra uses an audience scheme for some content and a topic scheme for others.

How Does Card Sorting Relate to Classification?

When you run a card sort, you'll see people organize their cards according to different schemes—sometimes they will use one scheme (often topic), and sometimes they will mix them up (some by topic, some by audience, some by task).

If you already have an idea that your content would suit one of the schemes, you can explore that in a card sort. You could, for example, ask people to determine what audiences the content items seem appropriate for and ask them to group the items accordingly.

Categories

Categorization is a fundamental human trait—people just naturally organize information into groups. Categories are an integral part of how we communicate.

If you are going to be organizing content into categories, it is handy to know about how our brains interpret them. Frequently, the way we think categories work is different than the way they actually work.

The Classical View

Western culture has developed a popular perception of how categories, groups, and concepts work. It is often labeled the *classical view,* and according to it, categories are clearly defined, mutually exclusive, and collectively exhaustive. In the classical view, categories have the following attributes:

- A category is a discrete entity defined by common properties of the members.

- Items are in the same category if and only if they have certain properties in common.

- Categories are abstract containers with things either inside or outside, and have clear boundaries.

- Categories exist independently of the people doing the categorization—that is, they exist in the world.

- No member of a category has any special status—all members are equal.

- All levels of a hierarchy are equivalents.

I've always struggled to create categories with clear definitions where everything fit neatly, because there would always be things that could go in two places or didn't quite belong. A few years ago, I discovered a volume of research that explored just how categories work, based on human cognition. And the light bulb went off for me—I have not thought about categorization in the same way since. I've outlined some of the main concepts here and also provided references at the end of the chapter.

First, let's look at one example to show that the classical view of categories doesn't always seem to work. Let's start with the category of game. *Game* is undoubtedly a category—a word representing a concept that is well understood by speakers of English. When I say *game* to someone, they have an idea what I mean.

Last year, I showed my daughter a set of images and asked her to choose the games. Figure 2.14 shows what she chose—cards, snooker, cricket, dominos, soccer, chess, jigsaw puzzles, a mother playing with a child, and a child playing pretend. I've shown this set of images to many people and most automatically respond that I'm showing them some games.

(ALL IMAGES COURTESY OF ISTOCKPHOTO)

FIGURE 2.14
Photographs
of games, as
chosen by my
daughter.

But look more closely at these games. There is little in common between soccer, chess, and a child playing pretend. It is difficult to define the common properties that could encompass such a broad range of activities. Does that mean my daughter and the people I've shown this photo to are wrong? Not necessarily.

I bet you thought for at least one of these pictures that "oh, that's not really a game." But I also bet that the game you excluded would have been included by someone else. The boundaries of the category of game are definitely not clear. Look at the dictionary definition of game. It goes on at length with many variations, and every dictionary has a slightly different focus. But despite the length of the definition, we have a clear idea what a game is, and the idea is fairly consistent between people.

Family Resemblance, Extendable Boundaries, and Central Members

The category of game illustrates some of the key attributes of categorization.

The first is the idea of *family resemblance*—just as some members of a family have similarities without being identical, so do objects in this category. Soccer and cricket are team sports; soccer, cricket, snooker, poker, and chess are all competitive; chess, jigsaw puzzles, pretend, and the mother and child are all learning activities; some are just for fun. None of these subgroupings defines the category, but rather each shows some of the ways objects resemble each other.

As new types of games emerge, they can be added to the category, and the *boundaries can be extended*—category boundaries are not fixed and immovable. I think we'd agree that some multiplayer online worlds are games, and can be added to the category even though they are relatively new.

Another attribute is that some objects fit in a category better than others— that is, there are *central and noncentral members*. For example, you can argue that chess and soccer belong to the category "games" better than a mother playing with a child. They are more central to the category.

Prototypical Items

Let's look at another example. Figure 2.15 shows three items that I hope we agree belong to the category of chair.

(ALL IMAGES COURTESY OF ISTOCKPHOTO)

FIGURE 2.15
Three chairs.

If I asked people to think of a chair, many would think of something like the kitchen chair. A kitchen chair is an example of a *prototype*—a best example of a category. Another example that is often used is the category of *birds*—robins and sparrows are prototypical birds.

This idea is similar to, and follows from, the idea of central members. But it goes beyond just the idea of some items fitting into a category better—a prototypical item is one that is not only central, but can actually represent, or stand in for, the category.

It is important to note that a given category does not have a single defined prototypical member; just that many categories will have a best example.

Basic-Level Categories

If I asked you what you were sitting on right now, I expect you would be more likely to say *chair* than *furniture* or *office chair*. If I asked you what is in the photo shown in Figure 2.16, you would be more likely to say *dog* than *Dalmatian* or *mammal*.

FIGURE 2.16
A mammal>dog>Dalmatian.

These examples represent the concept of a basic level of categorization. The classical view of categories suggested that all levels of a hierarchy are equal—that none is more important than the others. But much cognitive research has shown this not to be true—there is a level in the middle of a hierarchy that is better understood than other levels. George Lakoff says it well in his book, *Women, Fire and Dangerous Things*:[2]

---

2   Lakoff, G (1987). *Women, Fire and Dangerous Things: What Categories Reveal About the Mind.* University of Chicago Press.

*Categories are not merely organized in a hierarchy from the most
general to the most specific, but are also organized so that the
categories that are most cognitively basic are "in the middle" of
a general-to-specific hierarchy. Generalization proceeds upward
from the basic level and specialization proceeds down.*

—George Lakoff

Some of the characteristics of basic-level categories are:

- They are learned earliest.

- They usually have a short name in frequent use.

- People can name them quickly.

- A single mental image can reflect the category.

A particularly important aspect of basic-level categories is that they are not
absolute—we can't look at a hierarchy and definitively say what the basic
level is. They are relevant to individual experiences—a city-dweller may
have a basic level of "tree," whereas a country-dweller may have a basic
level of "oak." I often see this when talking about content with subject-
matter experts—they actually talk and think at a different level of detail
than us regular folks.

How Does Card Sorting Relate to Category Theory?

When working on any project that involves organizing content, you are
likely to come up against challenges that are, at their root, related to the
disconnect between the real world and the classical view. (Remember that
the classical view is not just an academic theory, but represents how most
people *think* categories work.)

I have worked on projects where people didn't understand why we
needed to do card sorting, or even make an effort to create an organization
scheme. They expected me to do it the *right way*—the one true way of
organizing the content. Often, their right way was the company structure;
sometimes, it was a technical aspect of the content. It can be quite hard to
convince them that there is no one right way and, in fact, that users may not

understand the way they are proposing. When you understand that there is a disconnect between classical theory and the real world, you may be able to communicate better with your clients and their users.

I've never worked on a project where I could come up with a perfect set of categories that was clearly defined with nice, neat boundaries. And I always have some sort of challenge when slotting content into categories—some always fits neatly, some only just fits, and some belongs to more than one category. But I don't expect it to work out perfectly. Instead, I aim to create a decent set of categories that suits the content as well as possible and makes sense to users. And, if I have content that fits into two categories, that's okay—in the digital world, we have that option.

But it's the idea of basic-level categories that I have found most useful and applicable for card sorting. When I choose content (this is explained in great detail in Chapter 5), I look for basic-level concepts and include those in the card sort (not too granular, not too broad).

Chapter 2 Summary/Tips

Card sorting is used as an input to information architecture projects—projects where you will be organizing information for other people to use. When you do this, you need to know about organizing, classification, and categorization.

Organizing can be harder than you think because:

- There is always more than one way to organize a set of information or things.

- Everyone thinks differently about how to organize information.

- How information will be used matters as to how it should be organized.

- Labeling is always difficult.

And there are many different classification schemes you can use:

- Topic

- Chronology

- Geography

- Alphabetical order

- Numerical order

- Audience

- Task

And then the human brain gets in the road and messes up your neat world:

- Categories actually don't have neat boundaries that are clearly definable.

- Some items represent a category better than others.

- There is a level of hierarchy that is more important than the rest—it is cognitively "basic," and we do most of our thinking there.

References

Lakoff, George (1987). *Women, Fire and Dangerous Things: What Categories Reveal About the Mind*. The University of Chicago Press.

Margiolis, Eric and Laurence, Stephen (eds) (1999). *Concepts: Core Readings*. The MIT Press.

Rosenfeld, Louis and Morville, Peter (2007). *Information Architecture for the World Wide Web: Designing Large-scale Web Sites* (3rd ed). O'Reilly.

Weinberger, David (2007). *Everything Is Miscellaneous: The Power of the New Digital Disorder*. Times Books.

Wright, Alex (2007). *Glut: Mastering Information Through the Ages*. Joseph Henry Press.

Case Study: Browsing for Barbie

Case study contributed by Dave Rogers, principal of UXCentric, Inc., an information architecture and user experience consultancy in Los Angeles, California.

Mattel recently asked me to revamp the information architecture of the Doll Showcase at BarbieCollector.comSM, its site for collectors of Barbie® dolls. A comprehensive gallery of more than 2,000 Barbie dolls and accessories, the Showcase was primarily organized around marketing-based themes that contained a number of Collections/Series. User research showed high appreciation for the Showcase, but visits were declining.

Mattel Producer Lou Esposito and I wanted insights into collectors' mental models of the Showcase. We also wanted to tap their collective expertise for ideas about reorganizing the Showcase. How do collectors organize their *own* collections? How would they like to browse the Showcase?

Card sorting was an ideal solution—but I couldn't expect anyone to sort more than 2,000 cards! I needed a smaller pool of dolls/cards that represented the broad sweep of collectible Barbie dolls. While surveying the Showcase, I discovered that the Fashion theme was a perfect subset. It contained about 130 dolls—a workable number for card sorting—organized into about two dozen Collections/Series (along with several uncategorized dolls). This provided the content for our first sort. For our second sort, we wanted to see if the Collections/Series within the Themes made sense to collectors. With just over 100 Collections/Series, we again had a reasonable number for a sort. We then recruited nine participants representing the range of Barbie doll collectors—from novice to committed.

The results were fascinating. For the first sort (dolls), we found little grouping consensus across *all* participants except when doll names provided hard-to-miss clues. The groups of the most avid collectors were remarkably similar, but did *not* mesh with the Collections/Series. Meanwhile, the groups of the less committed collectors were quite diverse. Serious collectors relied on their expert knowledge of *doll attributes* to sort, while the less experienced relied more on doll names/concepts and especially on the *feelings* that the doll names evoked.

Case Study: Browsing for Barbie (continued)

For the second sort (Themes), the groups were more dissimilar than similar, as all collectors grouped Collections/Series in a number of ways. This categorization suggested that Themes provided little guidance unless collectors specifically knew where a doll could be found—a fact confirmed by usability testing.

HOW CARD SORTING HELPED

The card sort and usability test results pointed us to the same conclusion—collectors browse for dolls in individual/personal ways. Relying on just one method severely hindered the users' ability to find what they were looking for.

FINAL OUTCOME

Our solution was to create a faceted navigation system. Collectors can now browse the Showcase by doll name, year of release, SKU numbers, Collector Labels™, and (for those accustomed to them) the existing Themes. Collector response is enthusiastic and demonstrated by an increased use of the Showcase.

Defining the Need

As I mentioned in Chapter 1, card sorting can help a project in many ways. So the first step in planning for a card sort should be to decide why you are doing it and what you want to learn. This simple step can have a big impact on how you set up your sort. Let's look at some situations and how they affect your approach.

Need to Learn Broad Ideas

Recently I've been working on many redesigns for large content-rich websites, like government websites and large corporate intranets. As I have a lot of experience with these types of projects, I often have clear ideas about how I'll organize the content. But every project is slightly different—I can't directly apply what I've learned from one project to another. And because I do a lot of short projects, I don't always know about the domain in depth.

In this type of situation, I use card sorts to learn about the domain, see what types of groups people form, and learn how they describe the content. The cards contain broad topics (not detailed pages), and I run face-to-face team card sorts. The biggest benefit from the card sort is hearing the discussions—the actual groups and card placement are secondary to that.

Need to Check You're on Track

I may have ideas about the organization of content, but I always want to check that what seems obvious to me will be obvious to someone else. For example, when I started managing the website for the Information Architecture Summit (iasummit.org/), I drafted a structure based on my own experiences, but wanted to make sure I was on track.

For this project, I asked a small number of people to do a card sort on just the basic information about the conference—it wasn't necessary to involve very many people or all the content. Nor was it necessary to plan for a lot of detailed analysis just to determine whether my ideas were okay.

Need to Explore an Idea in Detail

Occasionally I want to explore a small section of content in a lot of detail. I ran a second card sort for the IA Summit website—this time using detailed conference presentation titles. I wanted to find out how many different classification schemes people came up with, how many different groups they created, and what they put into those groups.

For this activity I knew I needed to involve many more people and really understand the results—I ran an online card sort with 30 participants and analyzed the outcomes using exploratory and statistical methods. (I use this example later in the book, so you can see how I analyzed it later.)

Need to Compare People

The folks at Etre, a London-based user research agency, had an interesting project[1]—they were engaged by Eurostar (a high-speed passenger train operating between the UK and Europe) to help redevelop its global web presence. Something they wanted to learn was whether audience groups thought differently about how to organize information.

To learn this, they decided to run an online card sort with 180 participants from three different audience groups in three different countries (and three languages). They planned up front to do both exploratory and statistical analysis. This approach worked very well, and they were able to see similarities and differences between audience groups.

Justify a Recommendation

Sometimes you know that you could get good results from a small card sorting study, but you also know that a small study won't convince those who need convincing.

In this situation, I think about how many participants I would normally involve to get the answers I want, and then I double it. I also prepare up front to do both qualitative and statistical analyses, even though I may feel like I need to do only qualitative analysis.

---

1   The full case study for this project is available from the book's website. See ꜰꜰ www.rosenfeldmedia.com/books/cardsorting/blog/ eurostar_card_sorting_case_stu/ for more information.

Setting Goals

You should spend some time thinking about what you really want to learn and how you want to use that information. If you are running a card sort for a client, quiz them about what they really want to learn.

I know this sounds sort of obvious, but this is the step that people often skip. It's easy to say "we should run a card sort" without really thinking through why you need to do so. When I work with clients, it can often be tricky to get them to think about what they want to learn. If you don't think about it up front, you might find that you learned things that were interesting, but ultimately of little value.

Here are some common goals:

- Learn about how people think about the content and main groups and use this information to create top-level categories and subcategories.

- Learn whether there are some high-level concepts in this content and use this information to better understand the relationships in the content.

- Involve website authors in a card sort of general web content as a way to show them that people think differently, and particularly to show them how other people think about their content.

- Explore whether there is one main classification scheme for this content or whether there is more than one. Use this information to guide whether to offer information in one way or many ways.

- Find out why a small section of the website is not working by exploring different methods of categorization. Use this information to decide whether to reorganize the content.

- Collect names to use for labeling content groups and categories.

When you've defined your goals, write them down and then write down what you hope to do with the information. Having your goals written down gives you an easy way to determine whether you've accomplished them.

Chapter 3 Summary/Tips

The first thing you have to do is figure out what you might want to learn. Everything else flows from this concept.

Here are some reasons why people might use card sorting:

- Learn broad ideas.

- See if they are on track.

- Explore an idea in detail.

- Compare how people think.

- Justify a recommendation.

Case Study: Understanding Your Audience

Sylvie Daumal (Paris, France)

I was asked to organize the information for a portal website aimed at young people. The content was information regarding school orientation plus activities in their local area, such as the following areas:

- Swimming pool information (name, address, opening hours)

- Swim training classes (time, price, subscription)

- Theater information (name, address, program)

- Theater classes (time, price, subscription, teacher, etc.)

- University information (name, address, fields)

- Program for each diploma (different levels)

We had many questions about how we should organize the content:

- Should we create categories for things like school, culture, art, and sports at the first level of navigation?

- Would it be relevant to create a distinction between swimming pool and swimming training?

- Should we create a distinction between the diploma levels (two-, three-, or four-year diplomas)?

We organized a card sort and learned some very useful information about the way that young people saw the world. They did not make a distinction between culture and sports, but they did see a difference between regular activities (like music classes every Wednesday) and events they could attend (like a rock concert). So in the first level of navigation, we created the categories called Activities and Going Out.

The second level for the activities was Art, Sports, Culture, and so on. In the Going Out section, the second level reflected the way they organized their schedule: small events they decided on the fly, events that needed to be organized a bit in advance, big events like weekend trips, and bigger ones like vacations.

Regarding school, during the card sort we noticed they didn't understand abstract words, but paid attention to the more concrete words. For example, when the label of the card was Tourism courses, they paid attention to Tourism. Students also tended to lump course work into field-related categories (such as, "I want to work in a hospital or in a school") rather than diploma-related categories (such as, "I want a three-year diploma"). We thus decided to organize the school section according to fields and, afterward, to display all the possible courses/diplomas related to that field inside the content part.

Card sorting was incredibly helpful because it gave us some very good insight about the way young people see their lives and organize their schedules (their mental models, in a sense). We were very confident afterward about our site map.

Choose the Method

T here are different ways to run a card sort and each gives you different outcomes. This chapter is all about the different methods—open or closed, team or individual, manual or with software. Before you choose the method, keep in mind that you need to determine your goals.

Open or Closed Card Sort

Among the first decisions to make is whether to run an open or closed card sort. As I mentioned in Chapter 1, "All About Card Sorting," you should use the following criteria to determine which one to use:

- In an open card sort, participants create and label their own groups of cards.

- In a closed card sort, you provide a set of categories and ask participants to slot content into those categories.

Open Card Sorts

Open card sorts are used much more frequently than closed because you can learn more from them—you get information about the groups people create as well as the cards that go into the groups.

An open card sort doesn't need to be completely free—you don't have to just let participants sort in a way that suits them. Depending on what you want to learn, you may decide to ask participants to focus on particular criteria. For example, you can ask participants to think about:

- Main audience groups

- Main tasks they are likely to do

- Steps or stages of a process

Participants then sort the cards according to that criteria.

Closed Card Sorts

Closed card sorts do not collect as much information as open sorts, mainly because you can't explore what kinds of groups people would create.

There are times, however, when you don't need to run an open sort. Use a closed card sort instead of an open when you have the following conditions:

- You have a set of categories that you know can't be changed, and you want to see where the content would go.

- You are adding a small amount of content to an existing structure.

- You are confident that your groups work well, and you want to explore a detailed aspect of content placement.

Like open card sorts, closed card sorts can be conducted for reasons other than to identify the location of content. They can be used as a communication tool, for consensus building, or as additional user research.

What You Can't Learn

I've heard closed card sorts described as a good way to check that a set of categories will help people find information. I think that's strange because during a closed sort you are asking people to put content into groups (classifying information), not asking them to look for information. Classifying content and finding it are dramatically different tasks. If you want to know where people would look for content, you should ask where they would look for it, not ask where they would put it.

Let me give you an example. I once helped a team who had run an open card sort on an intranet and created categories of *media releases, publications, guidelines, fact sheets,* and *policies.* They followed with a closed sort and users slotted content into these categories very easily. Based on my experience, I was confident these categories wouldn't work very well in the long term. To check, we asked people to look for information. For example, we asked, "Where would you look to find out how much travel allowance you are entitled to?" We quickly discovered that the categories created would not help users find the information they needed.

If you want to learn where people would look for information, that's what you should ask them.

Team Versus Individual Card Sorts

The next decision to make in planning a card sort is whether to involve participants individually or in teams. Not only does this decision affect the type and quality of data you are able to gather, but it also determines how well you will understand the decision-making process.

Team Card Sorts

I love team card sorts. During the card sort, the participants talk about what they are doing, argue about where various cards go, discuss different ways to group the cards, query what content means, and talk about how they might use the content. This discussion is incredibly valuable—in many cases, the discussion is more useful than the outcome of the card sort. In some of my projects, the best insights have come from these types of discussions.

> While their hands are busily shuffling the cards around, I learn all about what they hate about the current site, what they wish the new site would do, and how they never knew that particular utility already existed.
>
> —Torrie Thomas (Aquent)

The main disadvantage of a team sort can be group behavior. Sometimes a dominant member of a team can force his or her opinion on the others, and the outcome reflects the ideas of only one member. On the other hand, some teams make many compromises instead of working through their differences, and then the final outcome may not make a lot of sense to anyone.

Individual Card Sorts

Although I love team sorts, individual card sorts have their place as well. They are great for getting a larger number of responses, and it can be easier to coordinate individuals than teams.

The main disadvantage of individual card sorts is that you may not get the same insight into the process that went into the sort. If you are doing the card sort face-to-face, you can ask participants to "think aloud" during

the activity and explain why they are creating the groups. This captures some extra information, but has none of the rich discussion and banter that happens with a team sort.

Using Both Methods

When I can, I use both methods. From the team card sort, I learn about why people group cards as they do. From the individual card sort, I get more data from the same number of people.

It may be tempting to run individual card sorts with everyone doing the activity in a room at once—more information from the same number of people and less time required from you. I'd run team sorts instead—although it may take more of my time, the results would be better.

No matter whether you run a team or an individual sort, make sure that you are there to observe the process. In addition to listening to the discussions, you can also see the process people use to group cards—you can make note of which cards were grouped most easily, which were left until the end, and which were moved from one group to another.

Manual Versus Software

Individual sorts can be conducted with a card-sorting software tool or done with a physical set of cards. (Team sorts don't really suit a software tool.)

Manual

I prefer manual card sorting. I like the fact that it is low-tech and allows a wide range of people to be involved who may be less comfortable with a technical option. I also like the physical, spatial nature of the activity—spreading cards out on a table, putting things that are related near one another, and gradually putting them in piles is a very natural way to work, mirroring how we arrange our physical objects. This makes the activity intuitive for a wide range of participants.

Software

There are a number of tools for software-based card sorting. These look quite similar to a manual card sort—the "cards" look a bit like real cards and can be dragged around the screen into categories. The advantages of using software are the following:

- It is a one-step process. You do not have to enter the results from the card sort into a tool for analysis—the process of collecting the data enters it into the tool automatically.

- It can be much easier to involve remote participants.

- You may be able to involve more people than you would during a face-to-face sort.

Until recently, I never ran software-based card sorts because the tools were so poor. I worried that usability problems would get in the way of collecting good data. However, there are some new tools now available (described in the following section) that are easy to set up and use.

One way to combine the rich insight available from a face-to-face activity and the convenience of software-based sorting is to use screen-sharing software and a phone hookup. You can watch the participant work and talk to that person about what he or she is thinking.

Summary of Software Tools

Here are some examples of software tools that you might find useful. I've described the pros and cons, so you can pick the one that best suits your needs.

Optimal Sort

Optimal Sort (www.optimalsort.com/), illustrated in Figure 4.1, is an online browser-based tool that uses a drag-and-drop spatial interface. It caters to open and closed card sorts.

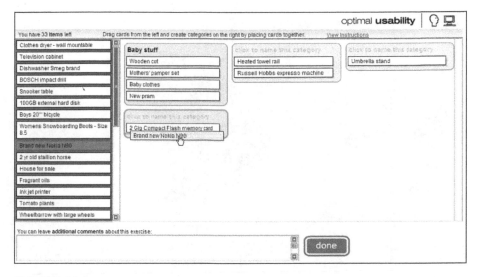

FIGURE 4.1
Optimal Sort's sorting interface.

There are a number of analysis options—you can export the data to my analysis spreadsheet (discussed in Chapter 9) or explore the results on the screen. Optimal Sort does not currently offer a statistical analysis option at the moment, but may do so in the future.

There are no limitations to the number of participants or cards, but you do need to think of how you are going to analyze the data, because many analysis tools have limitations (for instance, my analysis spreadsheet caters to a maximum of 40 participants).

Pricing is based on a subscription model with different prices for monthly, quarterly, and annual subscriptions. Small studies can be run free of charge.

WebSort

WebSort (websort.net/), shown in Figure 4.2, is another online card-sorting tool that is browser-based and runs over the Internet. It uses a drag-and-drop interface and a spatial sorting metaphor, and can include images on the cards. WebSort caters to open and closed card sorts.

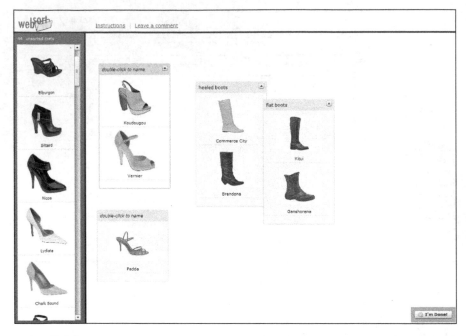

FIGURE 4.2
WebSort's sorting interface.

There are a number of analysis options that let you explore the results on the screen.

There are no limitations to the number of participants or cards.

WebSort is available as a monthly subscription. Prices currently vary from free to a couple hundred dollars depending on the subscription plan you select.

OpenSort and TreeSort

OpenSort and TreeSort (www.themindcanvas.com) are two tools in MindCanvas—a series of game-like elicitation methods for user research. OpenSort, shown in Figure 4.3, is for open card sorting; TreeSort is for closed card sorting. Both use an online browser and have a drag-and-drop interface.

You can perform analysis in conjunction with Uzanto (the company who provides the service), or you can do it yourself. Uzanto provides a visual analysis engine that allows you to play with the outputs without needing to know the statistics. A variety of statistical outputs are available.

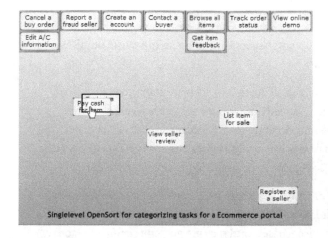

Singlelevel OpenSort for categorizing tasks for a Ecommerce portal

FIGURE 4.3
OpenSort's sorting
interface.

I haven't used this service, but I do like the look of the sorting interface and the visualization engine.

MindCanvas is priced on a project-by-project basis.

xSort

xSort (www.apple.com/downloads/macosx/productivity_tools/
xsort.html) is a software tool for MacOS (it does not run online). It uses a drag-and-drop spatial interface and caters to open and closed card sorts.

xSort is free software.

SynCaps

SynCaps (www.syntagm.co.uk/design/cardsort.shtml) provides computer-aided card sorting. It uses manual cards, printed with bar codes, to make the step of recording data easier.

The analysis options include proximity matrix, a simple dendrogram, and a text file that can be imported into Excel or a statistical analysis tool.

You do need to also purchase a hand-held barcode reader.

Chapter 4 Summary/Tips

The next step in preparing a card sort is to select a method:

- Open card sort or closed. Open is great for getting ideas on groups of content; closed is useful for seeing where people would put content.

- Team or individual. Team sorts are particularly good for learning information gleaned from the conversation a team has during the sort—sometimes more useful than the results themselves. Individual sorts are best used when you can't get everyone together in one place or when you want a large number of varied results.

- Manual or with software. Manual card sorts involve paper index cards, and people love them because they are low tech and not scary. Software-based card sorts are good for sending out to people who can't get to you.

CHAPTER 5

Choose the Content

W hen I started writing this book, I sent out a survey to colleagues that asked about their experiences with card sorting. One of the questions was, "Have you ever had a card sort go wrong?" There were a lot of funny anecdotes, but the most common reason for an unsuccessful result was poorly chosen content.

It is not good enough to grab a random assortment of different types of content from your website or to throw together a brainstormed wish list. You need to select content that is similar enough to make groupings meaningful, but diverse enough to represent the range of content or functionality you want to focus on. Don't "stack the deck" by selecting content that is likely to lead only to a particular result, but make sure the content you choose allows you to ask the questions you want answered. It's a classic case of getting out what you put in.

Locating Content

Your content source depends on the type of project you are doing—whether you are starting from scratch, redesigning an existing set of information, or exploring an idea.

Website from Scratch? Create a Wish List

If you are designing a site from scratch, create a wish list of all the types of information you will include on the site. List as much content in as much detail as possible. You may not know exactly what pages you'll end up creating, but you should be able to create a fairly detailed list of content ideas. Don't just use this wish list as the only source of content for your card sort, though—use the following tips for identifying additional content.

Existing Website? Start with a Content Inventory

If you are redesigning an existing site, you'll first need a thorough understanding of the current content. Otherwise, you won't know what you're missing. One starting point is a content audit or content inventory.[1]

---

[1] I've done more content inventories than a person should do in one lifetime. This article has spreadsheets, instructions, and links to more information about taking a content inventory: maadmob.com.au/resources/content_inventory.

An audit is based on a representative sample of content; an inventory is a full listing of all current content.

Whether you're using an audit or an inventory, the next step is choosing content to include in the card sort. Depending on the type of content you have, the type of website, and the size of the content set, you might choose the following:

- Topics or subjects

- Content pages from the website

- Products from a catalogue

- Navigation or index pages from the website

- Small sections of the website that you are confident belong together (for example, if you have large reports split into many pages, in most cases, you'll want to represent the entire report rather than individual sections or pages)

If you are working on a very large site, see the "Working on Large Sites" section later in this chapter.

Designing a System? Look to Tasks and Functions

If you are not working on a content-based website, but rather on a system or computer application, your content may include:

- Menu items for the application

- Key functions for the application

- Steps in a process

- Key tasks

Exploring an Idea? How to Begin

Sometimes you may want to do a card sort to simply explore an idea or topic. You can get ideas for content by:

- Brainstorming examples

- Seeing what is already available for that domain (for example, you might choose to examine all the relevant tags from a tagging-based system like Flickr or del.icio.us)

- Analyzing search queries

- Conducting a free-listing activity[2] with the design team or with users

Tips for Selecting Content

Selecting content for your card sort is not as obvious as it would seem. Here are some ideas for sorting content so that you will get the best possible results from your sort.

Select Content That Can Be Grouped

When I set up my first card sort for a very large intranet, I selected a random sample of pages from the existing intranet to use for the exercise. Luckily, I did a test run with a colleague before I took it to the larger group. I had chosen lots of individual pages from a large, diverse set, and even though there were 100 cards, there was not a lot of consistency or similarity between individual cards. My colleague was unable to create coherent groups out of this strange set of cards with unrelated content, and consequently was unable to provide much insight into how the content could be grouped on the site.

The content you use in the card sort has to be similar enough to suggest potential groupings. Check that each content item you will include on a card could have a potential partner (or many partners). You can choose to

---

2   In a free-listing activity, you ask users to list as many items as they can for a particular domain. See www.boxesandarrows.com/view/beyond_cardsorting_free_listing_methods_to_explore_user_categorizations.

leave some content items that don't have obvious partners in the deck in order to learn something about them, but these should be the exception rather than the rule.

On a recent sort, I deliberately included three cards I didn't really need. I was quite sure I would put them together in the final structure. But I put them in the deck so participants would have some cards that were easy to group—that they would easily spot and say "these go together." This gave participants the confidence to proceed to more difficult groupings.

> *It is important to have enough easy stuff to group so people don't feel stupid.*
>
> —Cathy Wells, Department of Agriculture, Fisheries, and Forestry (Australia)

Select Content That Is at the Same Level

I attended an information architecture workshop a few years ago and the presenter had a session on card sorting. His example involved a travel site and included cards like:

- Exhibition of local art
- Accommodations
- Science and technology museum
- Things to do and see
- Name of a particular zoo
- List of bed and breakfasts
- Upmarket hotels

These very different items were difficult to sort. "Accommodations" encompassed the idea of bed and breakfasts and hotels; the zoo, museum, and art exhibition were clearly "things to do and see." Naturally, participants placed the detailed cards under the cards that suggested broader categories and labeled the pile with the name of that category. At the end of the exercise, the presenter collated the results and showed how easy it was to get a clear structure from a card sort. I was polite for once and didn't point out the obvious flaw in the activity—without the broader cards, participants might still have come up with similar results, but they would not have been driven toward this particular result.

In order to avoid unnecessarily influencing the card sort in this way, content items you choose should be at a similar level. You can use very detailed content such as individual content pages or individual products, or much broader categories—subsections of a site or broad topics. Whichever you choose, don't mix the two.

Select Content or Functionality, Not Both

Another common mistake when selecting content to include in a card sort is mixing content with functionality, as seen in this list of cards from an intranet project:

- Travel policy

- Maternity leave provisions

- Installing new software

- Applying for leave online

- Procedures for purchasing office equipment

- Organizational chart

- Searching the intranet

- People finder

Participants were not sure what they should do with "searching the intranet," "applying for leave online," and "people finder." The consensus was that this functionality should be separated from the other intranet content and should be made available on the homepage.

Again, when choosing content for your card sort, try to make sure it is all of a similar type. If you still decide you do want to include functionality with content, it is sometimes possible to describe the functionality in such a way that it seems more consistent with the other terms (for example, "applying for leave online" could be "online leave system") or, conversely, to relabel content and functions as tasks.

Select Content That Is Representative

The content in the card sort needs to represent the content you will end up organizing. People create groups based on what you give them—if some content is not represented in the card sort, it will not be considered when creating groups.

> *The last card sort we did was aimed at the top levels of our library site, from the homepage down a level or two. Since our main goal was to see how the participants grouped items at these levels, we selected items that we anticipated would be either on these pages or accessed from these pages. We didn't have a formal methodology, just an educated selection.*
>
> —Brian Hoffman (Minitab Inc.)

Select Content That Does Not Lead the Activity

When selecting content, try to make sure that it doesn't lead participants to a particular result. In particular, be sure to watch for:

- **Overuse of a particular word.** Participants often put things together based on pattern matching of words, and a frequently used word gives them an easy (and potentially misleading) way to group content.

- **Words that represent a format such as *policy, manual, guide, fact sheet, or how to.*** It is too easy for participants to put these together without thinking about what the content is about.

- **Words that represent the current structure.** If participants already know the structure of the website, they are likely to re-create that structure in the sort.

Select Content That Participants Understand

If participants do not understand the content they are sorting, they are more likely to create groups based on surface characteristics such as word choice, rather than trying to decide what the content means in order to group similar ideas together.

> *I found we got much better results with the card sorts if we had the participants go through the stack of cards and ask about anything they didn't understand or were unsure of. That way they were sorting the cards based on the intent rather than possible misunderstanding of the terms. We were also able to take notes about the terms that were causing people problems and could revisit those later in a different study.*
>
> —Brian Hoffman (Minitab Inc.)

I mentioned before that for my first card sort for a big intranet I mistakenly chose content that couldn't be grouped. I fixed this problem by adding extra content for some topics and removing some content altogether. But my content set still attempted to cover the whole intranet site at once. When I took the card sort to participants, it still proved overly difficult.

In an organization with a broad range of responsibilities, participants from other areas or departments showed little interest in content outside their area of expertise. The result was that the sort had a lot of groups like *big corporate documents*, *newsletters*, *articles*, and *pages that belong to the "xxx" team*. These were valid groups to the participants, but what they really represented was "stuff that doesn't matter to me." That was a useful finding from the card sort, but it didn't give me good groups that I could use to help structure the intranet. If this is likely to happen to you, there are some ways to get around it:

- **Use different sets of content for different groups of people.** This works well if you know your audiences have particular interests.

- **Create a larger set of cards and tell participants to remove cards they don't understand.** It is far better to know that people are not interested in this content than to force them to sort it.

- **Focus on content that is relevant to participants.** Conducting a preliminary card sort with internal staff can give you an idea of some of the major groups and interests.

The danger, of course, is that people will say they aren't interested in anything at all (yes, this has happened to me). Use this as an opportunity to gather some more information by learning why the participant isn't interested. If possible, ask the uninterested participants to do some grouping on the parts they understand best.

> I didn't specify how many minimum piles an engineer was supposed to sort the deck into for a web/file navigation system. He sorted them into two piles: "$#*! I use" and "$#*! I don't care about."
>
> —Torrie Thomas (Aquent)

> We usually do a short content prioritization exercise right before the sort. This allows the participants to mark any unfamiliar terms and indicate what they find most important, and gives us a chance to clarify those terms while also getting at issues of terminology and/or jargon.
>
> —Dustin Chambers (UserWorks Inc.)

How Much Content/How Many Cards?

For most projects, I use between 30 and 100 content items (and therefore 30–100 cards). If you use fewer than 30 cards, there may not be enough overlap to create groups. More than 100 cards can be tiring to sort—it is hard for participants to remember what they have and where they have put them.

The time it takes people to do a sort has nothing to do with how many cards there are, but instead reflects how complex the content is. A 30-card sort with obscure or inconsistent content that doesn't fall naturally into natural groups takes much longer than a 100-card sort where the content is more straightforward.

You can use more cards (up to 200) in some circumstances:

- **Individuals can manage more cards than teams can.** Individuals can keep track of where the cards are more easily as they position them, and are not distracted by the discussion a team card sort creates.

- **If the content is easy to group, participants can manage more cards.**

- **Cards that cover broad topics that are clearly expressed are easier to work with than cards listing detailed content.** In general, topics are easier to understand than individual content items.

Working on Large Sites

Large projects, such as government or corporate websites and intranets, can make content selection challenging. Here are some tips:

- **Ignore some content.** Remember that you don't need to sort the entire site. If you already have good ideas for some areas of the site, exclude them from the card sort. For example, on a government intranet project, I already knew we were going to keep the core business content together and group it by topic, team, and then alphabetically. This allowed us to narrow the card sort down to key administrative information.

- **Sort small groups, not content pages.** Although there is some risk in creating small groups (you may create groups that users would not), this risk can be managed.

- **Use topics.** Identify the key topics or subjects within the site and use those instead of content. It takes additional work to identify the topics but provides good outcomes from the card sort. Topic ideas can come from an analysis of content, user research, or search terms. I did this recently for an 8,000 page site—although there was a lot of content, the set of topics was constrained and manageable.

- **Sort with overlapping sets.** Choose a large set of content—say 300 items that represent the whole content. Randomize them and create four card sorts each with 100 cards (overlap each group). This may be more difficult to analyze and sort, but it lets you cover more content and look at similarities and differences.

- **Conduct a few rounds of sorting.** Choose a subset of content and conduct a card sort. Discuss the outcomes with your team and determine what you would like to learn further.

- **Start with broad groups.** Based on your own ideas for major categories, select content in each category and conduct separate card sorts for each to identify the groups within a category.

Chapter 5 Summary/Tips

Content selection can just be hard, so spend a bit of time thinking about it.

- Make sure your content can be grouped. There's no point trying to get people to organize things that just don't go together.

- Make sure that you don't include detailed and broad content together. People will just put the detailed content "under" the broad.

- Don't mix up content and functionality. It just gets messy.

- Try your hardest not to lead to a predetermined result. You run a card sort to learn something new.

- Include terms and concepts people understand. If they don't understand it, they'll sort it by alphabet or some other useless method.

And if you are working with a large site:

- Remember that you don't need to do everything at once.

- Focus on a small area if you can.

- Sort on "topics" rather than detailed content.

- Run a few rounds of card sorts to explore more than a single sort.

Case Study: Creating Flexible Categories

Livia Labate (livlab.com)

While designing a web portal for users of a telephone service, our goal was to present the simplest possible interface that contained all the features that customers were able to access from their phones, as well as other enhanced features.

Our central business concern was to allow users self-service access to complex options, while keeping customer service calls to a minimum.

We started by interviewing potential users about their expectations regarding their service and current phone usage. This led to a task-analysis exercise, which provided insight into the overall user mental model, but it didn't address the specific user expectations for content organization and presentation.

The two things we wanted out of the card sort were an understanding of the hierarchy of content (which we had a notion of from the interviews) and the labeling of categories and content items.

One of our challenges was that for the first release of our site, only 50 percent of the content would be there, so it was important to create categories that could grow over time without being obscure or restrictive.

I was not confident we would be able to come up with these flexible categories, but we did. We included cards representing our best guess about future content—asking users to sort through a more complex scenario than they would normally be presented with at launch. After the sort, when we removed the content that wouldn't be there for the first release, we only had to make one category adjustment. Not bad for a card sort with over 130 items!

Later, during a paper prototyping session, we validated the groupings identified during the card sort by evaluating how successfully people found information in those categories and completed their tasks. Using paper prototyping to get feedback on the design, we also clarified labeling issues (category titles) that hadn't been completely clear to us during the card sort.

The card sort helped us to bridge the gap between our task analysis and paper prototyping, which allowed us to make a stronger case for a better solution than proposed by the other team, and ultimately created an interface that fulfilled user needs and ensured we kept those customer service calls to a minimum.

CHAPTER 6

Choose the People

This chapter gives you some ideas about who should facilitate your card sort and provides lots of tips for getting the right people involved as participants.

Choosing a Facilitator

The facilitator is the person who is going to run the activity (if it is done face-to-face). Chances are this will be you. Here are a few of the qualities that make a good facilitator:

- **Organized:** Card sorting involves a lot of little details, so it's important that the facilitator is on time, introduces the activity properly, and records the data.

- **Able to multitask:** Good facilitators can write notes, pay attention to what the group is doing, and anticipate questions all at the same time.

- **Enjoys working with people:** Participants work better if they are relaxed and the facilitator makes the activity enjoyable.

- **Good listener:** If the facilitator can't keep quiet and listen, or has to be at the center of attention all the time, he or she probably isn't right for this job.

- **Knows the content:** Participants often need to ask questions about the content listed on the cards and a good facilitator will need to know enough to clarify.

If you have never facilitated a card sort before, see if you can watch someone who has. Get this person to facilitate your card sort, or watch him run one of his own. If you can't do that, at least do a few practice runs with family or colleagues. A trial run will help you anticipate the flow of the activity and the types of questions people will ask.

Choosing the Participants

The best participants for a card sort are the end users of whatever you are designing. It is these people you are designing for, and your product will be more successful with their input. When you are thinking about whom you want to invite, try to find people who are interested in, and understand, the content. People who aren't interested in the content tend to rush through the sort without really thinking about their groupings.

Of course, you can run a card sort with people other than end users. You can involve team members, clients, and managers. But if you do so, think of their involvement as a communication activity—as a way of creating consensus or of clearly demonstrating that the internal team thinks differently from other user groups. If you involve the client, keep their results separate from the end users' results during analysis.

> We did card sorts with the client team and again with target users. Comparing the two results was interesting, and helped to sell the design process. However, since the client team was also a major audience, it highlighted compromises we would need to make.

> —Austin Govella (thinkingandmaking.com)

Organizing Participants into Teams

If you are planning on running a team-based card sort, try to involve people who know each other—that way, the team doesn't have to figure out who's who and how to work together. But be careful about the relationship of the people in the team. If you include managers and staff in the same team, staff will usually defer to the manager. Also, IT people are often intimidating to non-IT people.

Of course, it's not always possible to arrange teams into people who know each other. If your participants don't know each other, plan an icebreaker activity, some discussion of the product, or a practice sort before the main activity. This tactic allows the team to meet and set the group dynamic before attempting the main activity.

In my experience, the ideal team size is three. Three people work well together, can listen to each other, and can physically fit around a table to shuffle cards around. Four or five people can work successfully, but I've noticed that one or two of them tend to stand back and let the others do the work.

It is best with three people because then you can think better together. A big group doesn't really cooperate.

—My daughter Amber, a 10-year-old budding information architect

How Many Participants or Teams?

One of the most common questions I'm asked is how many people should be involved. The answer to this question depends on what you are trying to learn (which is why it is good to sort this out up front).

Naturally, the more participants you involve, the more data you have to help you make decisions. The trick is to involve a sufficient number of participants to learn what you need to, and not so many that you collect far more information than you need (which is a waste of participant input and harder to analyze).

Learn Broad Ideas or Determine Whether You Are on Track

When you need to get some broad ideas or check that your ideas are on track, you may need to run only a small number of card sorts—from 5–6 team or individual sorts, you can get some good ideas or determine whether you think in the same way as the participants do.

In this situation, a card sort should not be your only user research—make sure you use other methods to learn about your users as well.

Explore an Idea in Detail

If you need to explore an idea in detail, you need to involve lots of participants—enough that you can spot the areas where responses are consistent and where they differ.

Compare People

For some projects, you want to compare the results of different groups. For example, you may want to learn if there are differences between audience groups, age groups, or experience levels of users.

In this situation, you need to involve a lot of people. You must involve enough people within each group that you can identify a consistent pattern (or patterns) for the group and then compare them.

So, How Many Is Lots?

My experience is that there is no magic number for each type of goal— the biggest factor is the complexity of the domain and how well participants understand it.

Two of my recent card sorts offer good examples (both of these examples are in Chapters 9 and 10, so you can see detailed results there):

- When I teach information architecture workshops, I run a card sort. The context is a tourism website for a wine region, and I use around 40 cards. As the topic is fairly straightforward, participants always create very similar groups. By the time I ran the first six card sorts, I can spot very consistent patterns—additional card sorts don't add anything new.

- I recently ran a card sort using presentations from the Information Architecture Summit, using 99 cards. Even after 30 participants, there was very little consistency. Even if I tripled the number of participants, there would still not be a consistent outcome—there are just too many ways of organizing this content.

In a situation where you need to involve lots of people, start with 10 participants or teams. (If you are comparing groups of people, involve 10 of each type.) Then do a preliminary analysis and make a decision about whether you have enough information. You may learn that you need more data, or that you need to refine your card sort to better achieve your goals. Don't be afraid to change the card sort if you aren't getting what you need. It is better to change it and achieve your objectives than to continue with something that isn't working.

How Many Participants Does It Take to Be Significant?

I often see discussions and studies[1, 2] about how many participants are needed to get "statistically significant" results.

This makes sense in an academic or scientific research project where you must prove that your conclusions are valid and that results from a subset of people represent the larger group. But I don't believe it is particularly relevant for information architecture projects.

As I've mentioned earlier, in an information architecture project, card sorting is most helpful for identifying the types of groups people create, what they put into groups, and how they describe those groups. This is but one input of any project—you will also use your overall project goals, other user research, and an understanding of content to design an information architecture.

Of course, you want to get good quality results from your card sort, but that comes from good planning, good content selection, and involving the right participants. It doesn't come from getting enough people to achieve statistical significance.

Enlisting Participants

Another very common question is "Where do I find participants?" As you can expect, there is no magic answer to this—it depends on the type of project and your relationship with existing users.[3]

A few years ago, I worked almost exclusively on intranet projects. One of the biggest benefits of working on an intranet is that it is very easy to get in contact with users because they are members of the company. I've used many methods for inviting people, such as using internal networks, randomly selecting people from a staff directory, and choosing people from individual work areas or role types.

---

1   Nielsen, J. (2004). *Card Sorting: How Many Users to Test.* Alertbox. 2006.

2   Tullis, T. and L. Wood (2004). *How Many Users Are Enough for a Card-Sorting Study?* Proceedings UPA 2004, Minneapolis, MN.

3   Mike Kuniavsky's book *Observing the User Experience* has a detailed chapter about recruiting people for user research studies, with many tips and tricks.

For website projects, if you already have a good relationship with a core group of users or key stakeholders, start with these people. If your website is important to them, they may be quite happy to help you out.

If you don't have regular contact with users or are working on a website without an existing user group, here are some tips for enlisting participants:

- Ask family, friends, and colleagues if they know anyone who fits the characteristics of your users.

- Involve a recruitment or market research company—they may have potential users on their client list.

- Talk to your call center or help-desk staff—they may know some regular callers or may be able to ask callers if they would like to be involved.

- Advertise on your website or in the company newsletter.

- If you are demonstrating your product at a conference or trade show, run a card sort at your stand—keep it short and simple and offer an incentive for people to get involved.

Whatever you do, invite people personally. Don't send bulk, unsolicited email (otherwise known as *spam*) to people.

No matter what the type of project, I have found that people are usually quite happy to do a card sort. It is an easy activity, doesn't need to take up much time, and they can often see how the results are relevant to them.

Inviting Participants

When you invite people to be involved in your card sort, you need to make sure they know what they will be involved in and answer their questions beforehand.

I like to let people know:

- What the project is about.

- What a card sort is about.

- How the card sort is used in the project.

- Who they'll be working with.

- How long it will take.

- That they don't need any special knowledge or preparation.

The following sidebar shows a sample script I have used many times when inviting participants.

Sample Script

We ([the team]) are currently redesigning the [name] website. An important part of the project is to make sure people can easily find information they need. One way we learn about this is to do an activity called a *card sort*, and we'd like you to be involved.

We will be giving you a set of index cards that show information on the website and asking you to sort them into groups. We can then look at how you think about the information groupings and how information could be organized.

[You will be working in a small team with names/description.]

You don't need to have any special knowledge, don't need to do any preparation, and there are no right or wrong answers.

The card sort will take less than an hour. [Add logistical details—where to show up and such.]

Chapter 6 Summary/Tips

The question I'm asked most often is who to involve in the card sort and how many to involve. When thinking this through, remember:

- Involve actual users, not managers, internal staff, or substitute users. The point of a card sort is to learn about how your real users think.

- You want enough participants so you can get a range of answers and see similarities and differences.

- Statistical significance is completely irrelevant for information architecture projects, so don't even worry about it.

- There is real benefit in listening to a team work together and discuss the card sort, so run team sessions rather than individual ones—go for quality, not quantity.

- Don't collect more data than you need—you'll just have trouble analyzing it.

Make the Cards

A fter all the hard work of figuring out what you want to learn, choosing content, and arranging people, the process of creating cards is relatively simple.

If you will be running a physical card sort, you'll need to make up a bundle (or bundles) of cards. If you will be running a software-based sort, you don't need to make cards, but you will need to get the cards into the software system. Either way, the most important part of this process is writing good titles that are easy to understand and represent the content well.

Making Physical Cards

Most people conduct manual card sorts using the index cards that are easily available from an office supply store. I use 3" × 5" (76mm × 127mm) cards. They are easy to handle and have enough room to list the content. I print the content onto copier labels and stick them on the cards, as shown in Figure 7.1. This makes producing multiple sets of cards very easy.

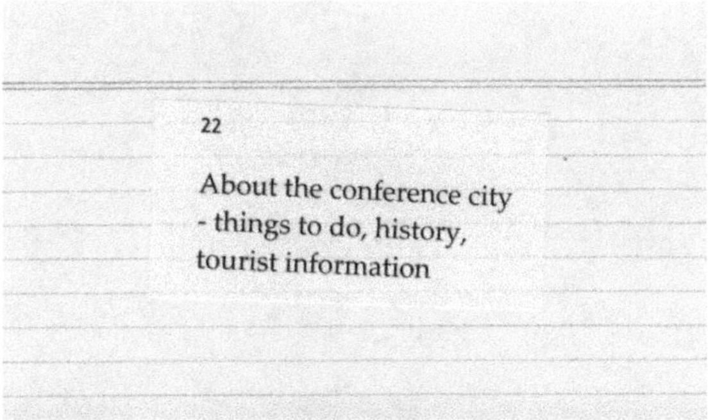

FIGURE 7.1
A physical index card with a label stuck on.

22

About the conference city - things to do, history, tourist information

My Analysis Spreadsheet

I use a spreadsheet for analysis, further discussed in Chapter 9. The spreadsheet has a list of card titles, which I then use to generate sticky labels.

The analysis spreadsheet and instructions are available at ♠ www.rosenfeldmedia. com/books/cardsorting/blog/card_sort_analysis_spreadsheet/.

Other good ways of preparing cards are by using the following:

- **Printable sheets of cards.** These are often sold for business cards. The individual cards are smaller than index cards but still large enough to handle.

- **Handwritten cards.** Write the content straight onto the cards. This is fine for small card sorts but becomes tedious for anything large.

> *I ran a card-sorting exercise where the person preparing (hand writing) the cards for me didn't check the spelling of the words. It gave the participants a giggle but they did notice the spelling errors!*
>
> —Ruth Ellison (ruthellison.com)

Believe it or not, you don't need to use cards for a card sort. A colleague recently told me about a card sort where she printed pages of existing content (she cut off navigation elements) and ran the sort with actual content. It was slower than a regular card sort, as participants delved into the details of some of the content, but it gave good results as they understood exactly what they were sorting.

What to Put on Cards

For most card sorts, the card contains just a short title. The title should have the following criteria:

- Be easy for participants to understand

- Accurately represent the content

- Spell out any acronyms and jargon

Occasionally, a title won't be sufficient, and you need to include more information such as a fuller description of the content, an image, or some paragraphs about the content.

We recently did a card sort without descriptions (someone else prepared the cards), and the resulting data was strange. When we reviewed with the client, he couldn't understand why several of the items were placed where they were. We eventually found out that several of the items had titles that didn't match the content/function. So we had to rework the data and retitle a bunch of items.

—Todd Zaki Warfel (toddwarfel.com)

Example: Creating Good Card Titles

Creating good titles isn't as easy as it might sound. When I prepared a card sort for the IA Summit conference information, I asked a friend to do a test run for me. What happened wasn't pretty—he found it very difficult to make sense of the content and then create groups with it.

It wasn't his fault, though. I had prepared the cards in a rush without thinking much about the titles (ignoring all my own advice). And I assumed he knew something about card sorting and the IA Summit, so I didn't take the time to introduce the activity properly and give him the context he needed.

I fixed the cards and asked him to do it again, explaining the activity and context properly. The second time around went much more smoothly. The improvements to the cards were subtle. I removed some duplicates (*conference venue* and *conference venue facilities* look the same, even though I had a clear idea of the difference in my head), clarified jargon (*papers* and *sessions* are jargon if you're not involved in organizing conferences), and expanded most of the titles to better explain the content. Some of the changes are shown in Table 7.1.

Can you see the difference? Even though the changes aren't dramatic, it is much easier to understand what the card means and what the content represents. The revised content is much easier to sort because it is easier to understand.

TABLE 7.1 CLARIFYING CARD TITLES

Before	After
About the IA summit—general overview	About the IA summit—general information
Call for papers	Call for proposals
Regular session schedule	Timetable for main conference presentations
Speaker bios—regular sessions	Speaker bios—main conference presentations
Getting from the airport to the venue	How to get from the airport to the conference venue
Social activities	Social activities that accompany the main conference
About this year's IA summit	About the 2006 IA summit—theme and aims of the conference

Closed Card Sort: Making Category Cards

If you are doing a closed card sort, you'll need a set of cards for your predetermined categories. As with the main set of cards, you can write them by hand or print sticky labels. Whatever you do, make sure the category cards look different from the main cards so that participants don't get the two confused. You can use different colored cards, write the category name in capital letters or write it by hand, or use large sticky notes.

Making "Cards" Using a Software Tool

Good titles are just as important for a software-based card sort as they are for a physical card sort. But before you go too far with your titles, check the allowed length of the title and how it displays on-screen.

Then you need to get your card titles into the software. Again, determine how this works before you start. With some tools, you may be able to import data from a spreadsheet, while with others you may need to type the titles by hand.

Chapter 7 Summary/Tips

Making the cards is quite straightforward:

- $3'' \times 5''$ index cards are a good size to handle and easy to source.

- Pay attention to your titles; sloppy titles make for a bad sort.

- Get someone uninvolved in the project to check your titles before you print the cards.

Case Study: A Tale of Two Sorts

Donna Spencer

My first large-scale card sort was an intranet redesign for an Australian government department. Everything was new to me at this point. I had never led a project of this type, designed a site this big, worked with a content management system, and had only used card sorting once (on a smaller scale). I should have been terrified but I was too naïve.

The intranet had around 10,000 pages of content. Each area of the department had its own "site" to use however they liked and each had a different look. The main problem was that, because the content was organized by departments, staff couldn't find the information unless they knew who was responsible for it.

I started the project with a content inventory and an extensive set of staff interviews. This worked out very well—staff were interested in getting involved and did want a better intranet. I learned a lot about what the intranet needed to do well.

I wanted to run a card sort and started to plan the content selection. That became tricky because I wanted fewer than 100 cards, representative of all the content on the intranet and quite detailed. (I also wanted individual content pages as I thought using small groups would lead the result.) It was almost impossible. I first tried to select every 100th line of the content inventory. That didn't work—some small sections were skipped and some large sections had too many cards. I tried getting 100 random cards, which also didn't work. In the end, I just hand-selected what I thought were the main items of content.

I cold-called 20 people across the department. I made up four bundles of cards, delivered each to the participants one day, told them what to do, and picked up the cards the next day. I jotted down the results on a piece of paper and delivered the cards to someone new until everyone had finished.

Then I had to analyze the data. I started to enter it manually into one of the card-sorting tools, but that was much too slow and painful, so I included it all in a spreadsheet in much the same way I've outlined in Chapters 9 and 11 in this book.

Case Study: A Tale of Two Sorts (continued)

I was horrified. The nice outcome I had hoped for just wasn't there. Some participants weren't able to complete the sort well—the content was so diverse that they had trouble making groups. Some people had organized the cards by who looked after it. Some organized it by document type (how to, publications, policies). Some had organized it topically, but the topics they chose were all different. It was so mixed up that I didn't really analyze it properly.

I designed a new structure. It was mostly based on the card sort and some other ideas from the user research (yes, I made it up). I ran a usability test, which went fairly well, and made some small changes.

The real troubles started later in the project, when we were starting to explain the changes to the employees. Although the structure had tested okay, many people hated it. They didn't like how it was grouped and labeled. I justified the structure based on the card sort. For example, I had created groups called Services, Computing, and Training. These labels came directly from the card sort so I thought they were okay. In reality, people weren't sure what Services meant (I should have spotted that when analyzing), they hated the word Computing, which felt old-fashioned, and Training was definitely not in vogue (one person in that team said, "you train dogs, not people"). I made changes and the intranet launched.

Looking back, I made three big mistakes:

- I made decisions based on a surface analysis without thinking about underlying causes.

- I read too much into the card sort—believing that the groups people created were what they *wanted* (see Chapter 11 for more about this problem).

- I let myself be led by an activity instead of doing good deep thinking.

Although it was frustrating at the time, I learned more from my mistakes than I would have from success, but I don't want to repeat the experience.

Case Study: A Tale of Two Sorts (continued)

WHEN BAD SORTS GO BETTER

The next large-scale card sort I did was a while after the first, and again for an intranet. Learning some lessons from the first, I did quite a few things differently.

The first difference was that I worked much more closely with a team, rather than on my own. This made a huge difference in the project—three heads were definitely better than one.

Instead of trying to make the card sort cover all intranet content, we excluded two large sections. We had ideas for that content and didn't need to explore anything in the card sort. That made a big difference also, as we were able to get good coverage of the content with 100 cards.

We ran the card sort as facilitated team sessions, and two of us observed every sort. When we couldn't meet face-to-face, we posted cards and instructions to participants. This gave us great insight from team sessions, plus a lot of data from the individual sorts.

We put the card sort results into a big spreadsheet and printed it. We also printed key insights from our earlier user research. We locked ourselves in a meeting room for two days with two whiteboards, lots of markers, and snacks, and worked together to create the new intranet structure. The card sort was useful, but not more influential than user interviews, intranet goals, and content analysis. We mostly used the card sort to identify broad groupings and ideas about labeling. After testing the structure and making some minor changes, we designed the navigation method and page layouts for the intranet.

This was an ideal project. The new intranet structure was accepted fairly well by the staff, was easy to implement, and is working well even a few years later. I put this down to teamwork and having good input to guide our decisions.

CHAPTER 8

Manage the Sort

If you have been following the steps in the previous chapters, you are almost ready to run your card sort. This chapter outlines a few bits and pieces you need to do before you start, and how to facilitate the actual sort.

Prepare for Analysis

The last step in your planning process should be to figure out how you will analyze the results from your card sort. You don't want to collect a lot of data without first knowing what to do with it. Jump ahead to the analysis chapter to get an idea of the options and choose your approach.

Double-check that your plan will provide the data you need. For example, ask yourself the following questions:

- If you are going to invite 60 people and want to do mainly qualitative analysis, how will you manage that volume of data?

- If you're leaning toward statistical analysis, have you invited enough people to get good results?

- Does the analysis tool have restrictions that affect what you do? Most statistical tools require that each card is in one place only, and some have restrictions on the number of cards and participants.

Other Supplies

If you are running a manual card sort, make sure that you have spare index cards (to allow participants to duplicate or create their own content), sticky notes (for writing labels describing the groups), rubber bands (to bundle cards), and pens (see Figure 8.1).

FIGURE 8.1
The essentials: cards, sticky notes, and markers

Before You Start: The Test Run

Sometimes I get caught up in a project, put a card sort together, arrange participants, and go out and run the activity at the last minute without testing it first. Every time this happens, I wish it hadn't. A test run is the last chance to make sure you have planned your card sort well so that it will give you the results you need.

Really, I cannot stress enough how important a test run is. I have never done a test run where everything worked perfectly—I always find something I'm glad I can fix. The things I usually spot in a test run are

- Badly worded instructions

- Duplicate content

- Titles that don't describe the content well

- Misspelled card titles

- Cards that can't be grouped

Somehow, I never manage to spot these in the spreadsheet or document.

The first step is to test the card sort by doing it yourself—that will help you spot the most obvious errors. Then test the card sort with another person—perhaps someone on your team or a manager. Test your introduction as well to make sure you have answers to questions ready.

If you will be using a software tool to conduct the sort, make sure you test that too. For browser-based tools, check that they work with the necessary web browsers. For installed products, check that they have been installed where needed.

If you will be using a spreadsheet or software tool to record and analyze results, record the results for at least one sort. Do both data entry and analysis. You don't want to find out that you have problems with your software after you have collected data. For the IA Summit card sort I mentioned in the last chapter, I used 99 cards and then found out one of the statistical analysis tools I planned to use allowed only 80. I really, really wasn't happy about that.

Run the Card Sort

You've planned, prepared, and tested and the big day has arrived—you're ready for your card sort. This section mainly covers the steps in a face-to-face (or facilitated software-based) activity. In a remote software-based activity, there is little to do except wait for the responses to come in.

The steps for running a card sort include:

1. Introduce the activity.

2. Hand out cards and materials.

3. Participants sort the cards.

4. Participants label the cards.

5. Ask follow-up questions.

6. Record the outcomes.

Introduce the Activity

The first part of the card sort is to introduce the activity—explain to the participants what it is all about and what you expect of them. A sample introduction script is shown on page 98.

Provide Context

Providing the context is extremely important as it influences how participants approach the activity and think about the content.

In providing the context, be sure to do the following:

- Give enough background information that participants understand what the cards are about.

- Avoid leading participants to a particular result.

- Avoid long explanations.

- Steer people toward creating groups.

- Steer people away from designing the whole website

I've tried many ways of introducing card sorts. My current approach is to tell participants the following information:

- That the activity is for a website or project.

- What is on the cards.

- That I would like them to create groups of cards that make sense to them to go on the website.

- That they don't need to worry about creating hierarchies, designing navigation, or creating cross-links.

- Then I reinforce that I would *really like them to create groups of cards and that I'll do the hard work of designing the structure of the website.*

I've heard a lot of stories about participants who are told the card sort is for a website, and then they start designing all sorts of functionality and other things for the website. If this happens, just remind them that what you really want is for them to create groups.

> Participants can get carried away trying to put the sort in the context of a website. I've seen them place elements on the table as they would be positioned on-screen, talking about drop-down menus and diverting attention away from content categorization.
>
> —Dustin Chambers (UserWorks Inc.)

Some teams, particularly those with participants who have designed websites before, want to create the perfect hierarchy. They start talking about things being subgroups of other things, some being broader and more detailed. I usually discourage them from worrying too much about the hierarchy and focus just on what content makes good groups. I tell them that they don't have to create the hierarchy—that I'll be putting together the results from all the activities and doing the sort.

An Introduction Script

My sample introduction is listed in this sidebar. I have used this many times for team card sorts and software card sorts.

WHAT THIS IS FOR

We [the team] are currently redesigning the website for [company]. An important part of the project is to make sure that people can easily find the information they need.

WE'RE DOING A CARD SORT

The activity we would like you to do is a "card sort"—we give you a bunch of index cards that show information on the website, and you sort them. We can then look at how information could be organized and how other people think about information groupings.

WHAT YOU HAVE TO DO

The cards contain headings for types of information that may be included on part of the website. They may not cover everything that will eventually be included.

We would like you to sort the index cards into groups of cards that, to you, belong together. You may like to think about this information:

- What content would you like to see together on a website if you were looking for some of this information?

- Are there different things you need to know at different times?

- What cards just seem to belong together?

One classic example I had recently was a guy who spent 2.5 hours filling a massive boardroom table. Not only was there a hierarchy of groups, but also relevance was indicated by proximity, and importance/priority by order down the table. It was a 3D card sort. I strongly suspect that this happened because he was told the exercise was for a website, rather than some more generic purpose.

—Patrick Kennedy (www.gurtle.com/ppov/)

An Introduction Script (continued)

There is no right or wrong way to group the cards.

If you have this situation:

- Cards that don't fit with anything, then leave them out.

- Cards that you would never be interested in, then group them together and leave them out.

- A card that you would like to put in two places, then write its name on a spare card and put it in both places.

- A large group, then see if you need to break it into smaller subgroups.

- Lots of small groups, then see if you can group them into a larger group.

When you have finished grouping the cards, place a sticky note on top and describe why you have put them together—a few words is enough. Bundle the groups with elastic bands so we can tell which cards go together.

WHAT HAPPENS NEXT

We look at the different ways that people group the cards. This helps us to see which topics clearly belong together and which ones don't. We also look at the way people describe their groups and this helps us to create labels (such as for navigation) on the website.

Anticipating Questions

There are two questions that come up so often, it is worth planning for them and mentioning them in the introduction.

Can I Put a Card in More Than One Place?

The question I hear most often is, "Can I put a card in more than one place?" This happens when participants think a card could go in more than one group, and they do not feel strongly enough either way.

Given that what you want to learn from card sorting is potential groups of content, and given that the real world never falls into clear categories anyway, I suggest you allow this. Allowing cards to be categorized in more than one way lets participants sort into groups that feel natural for them and stops them from worrying about forcing cards to fit. It also provides you with very useful information about content that may overlap categories.

Have some blank index cards handy and ask the participants to write out extra cards when this happens.

The disadvantage of allowing cards in more than one place is that analysis tools don't manage it well. Card-sorting software tools don't allow it at all, and many statistical analysis techniques are based on the premise that cards will be in only one place. If this is true for you, ask the participant to identify the category he feels is a better fit, use this for analysis, and make a note of the alternate category.

How Many Groups Should I Make?

Sometimes participants ask how many groups they should make. I tell them to make as many as make sense given the content—but that two is too few and 100 is too many.

I know that some facilitators give participants a precise number of groups, usually based on the idea that there are only so many navigation items they can fit on a screen. I don't think this approach yields the best results. Given that you will be combining the findings with the outcomes from other activities such as user research and content analysis to create the final categories—and will not take categories directly from the card sort—specifying the number of groups is not necessary.

Hand Out the Cards

Once you've finished the introduction, hand out the cards. (If you hand out the cards before the introduction, people will start looking at them and not listen to you.)

It's the little things that make a difference, and this is one place where a little detail makes a big difference. If you hand people a tight bundle of cards, most will look at the cards one at a time and start to make groups as soon as they can, without an idea of what is coming up in the card bundle. Most people won't go back and reorganize their content based on later cards.

If you spread the cards out on a table and encourage people to look at the set before starting, they will create much better groups. If you are running a team sort, make sure that everyone has cards in front of them so everyone is able to get involved.

If you are using the same set of cards more than once, make sure the cards are well-shuffled between participants, or they will just follow the same pattern as the previous people. That sounds obvious, but I bet we all make this mistake from time to time.

Observe the Sort

Most card sorts require little facilitation once they get started. Your job at this point is to observe what happens, and answer questions about content or how they should approach the activity.

Keep an eye out for group-management problems, such as one person dominating, some people not getting involved, or some people always being ignored. If you notice the group isn't working well together, intervene as inconspicuously as you can. If one person is being dominant and others are not contributing, you can address the quieter members directly and ask what they think of the results so far. Or you can listen to a comment by a quieter member and repeat it so it is heard by the group.

The most important thing is to listen to the discussion. Make notes of the ways people describe what they are doing. Teams will frequently say, "Well, this is *about* such and such." The *about* descriptions are very useful—they give you ideas as to why a group of content exists and the ideas people discard. I once ran a team card sort for a client and noticed that every team at some point said, "This is all the *agriculture* stuff," but they didn't write the word agriculture in the label. But, because they had all talked *about* agriculture, we were confident it would be a good label.

It is also valuable to make notes about cards that are put together first and those left until last. The cards put together first (and that stay together) will usually represent straightforward natural groups that you can be confident will work well. The cards left until the end usually represent content that doesn't fit into groups as easily.

Sometimes participants make interesting spatial groups. A small, tight group of cards may represent a group that is conceptually similar, while a spread-out group may represent a broader concept. Cards in the center of the group often represent best or prototypical examples of that group. If you spot an interesting spatial pattern, take a photo of the table and think about what the layout represents during the analysis step.

If possible, make an audio recording of the session and produce a rough transcription after the session, focusing on capturing the *abouts* and other keywords. As I mentioned earlier, in some situations this is more useful than the final outcome of the card sort.

Labeling the Groups

As you see the team start to settle on a set of groups, encourage them to have a look at their groupings and to write labels.

I don't usually tell participants that they will need to create labels when I introduce the activity because people may behave differently if they know they will be expected to explain their decisions later. I have noticed that if I tell them they will have to label, they start thinking of names early, rather than thinking about groups—it is subtle, but when people think about labels, they are less likely to explore different ways of grouping content.

Participants can write a rough description of why the cards are together or provide a concise label (see Figure 8.2). A rough description is often quite interesting, as it provides more insight than a short label. It can, however, be harder to analyze and doesn't give you a neat set of labels you can eventually use in the site.

FIGURE 8.2
Writing a label for a group.

Debriefing

At the end of the activity have a look at the groups that were created and
ask some follow-up questions:

- Ask the participants about the *overall rationale* for their grouping
  approach. This helps you to understand whether their card sort uses an
  underlying approach or whether they have just made rough groups.

- Ask participants to point out the *best examples* from each group. There
  will often be one or two cards that represent the group best and other
  cards that are less representative. This is very handy for when you are
  creating the final structure.

- Find out *if the team is happy* with the overall outcome—many teams
  will have compromised on many parts of the result. It is handy to know
  whether people are committed to what they have created. For example,
  if everyone is uncommitted, you will not be able to rely on the results.
  If they are all happy, you know it is a good outcome.

- Also ask about the *easy and hard parts* of the activity. Although you may have observed it, it is useful to know what the participants thought was easiest and hardest.

At the end of the activity, let the participants know that you will combine the outcomes of their session with that from other sessions and other research, and will use it to structure the information. If you are creating a report, find out if they would like to receive it. Often people are interested in knowing what other teams did and how you used their activity.

Record the Outcomes

It is important to record the outcomes of the card sort as soon as possible—the last thing you want to do is to drop a bundle of cards and lose your data.

I always give sticky notes to participants to write their labels on, and I always have a number on each card (for my analysis spreadsheet). At a workshop recently, someone came up with an incredibly simple way of recording the outcomes—to write the relevant card numbers straight onto the sticky notes (see Figure 8.3). It was such a great idea. I can just grab the sticky notes and reuse the cards immediately without losing the results.

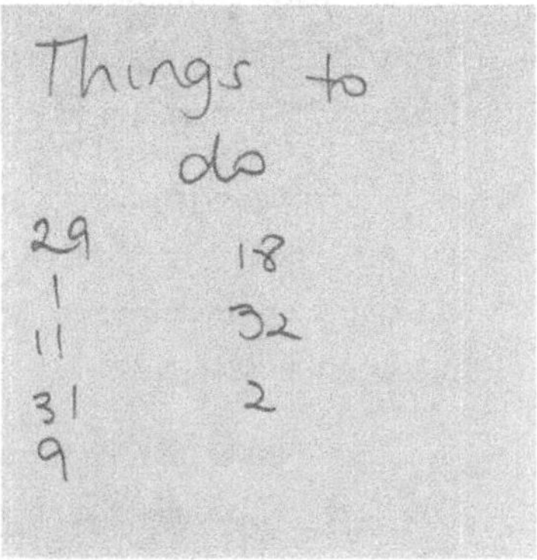

FIGURE 8.3
Card numbers are written straight onto the sticky note used for the label.

The next step is to get the results into your analysis tool. How you do this depends on the tool you are using. I have set up my analysis spreadsheet so I can quickly enter the card number and group name—this takes only a few minutes for a small sort and even a card sort with 200 cards takes less than 15 minutes (see Figure 8.4). If you are doing a physical card sort but using a software tool for analysis, see if there is an easy way to load the data. For many tools, you might have to enter each participant's results individually.

	A	B	C
1	Card no	Group	Card name
2	9	Activities	Glow-worm caves - tour details, costs and t
3	31	Activities	Heritage walk - details of a local walk to see
4	1	Activities	Sunday arts & crafts market
5	4	Activities	Historic library - location and opening hours
6	18	Activities	Winery bus tour - full day
7	32	Activities	Winery bus tour - half day
8	13	Events	Application form for the 2007 wine show
9	22	Events	Winners from the 2006 wine show
10	3	Events	Annual wine show - date and location
11	29	Events	Harvest feast - March every year, wineries de
12	11	Events	Winery walkabout - annual event with special
13	2	Events	Live music at the pub - schedule of bands
14	16	Wineries	7th island (vineyard, winery, cellar door) - loc
15	28	Wineries	Dog leg (winery & cellar door) - location, oper
16	34	Wineries	Gooda wines (vineyard & cellar door) - openin

FIGURE 8.4

My card-sorting analysis spreadsheet makes entering results easy. Enter the card number and the group; the card name fills in automatically.

If you are using a software tool, your data is recorded for you. Check that you have what you expect before you get into analysis. (I once used an online tool that lost data. I knew about it only when someone wrote to me and gave feedback.)

Chapter 8 Summary/Tips

This is where your planning and preparation come together, so don't rush it. Take your time and remember the following tips:

- **Do a test run.** If you choose to ignore everything else I have written, please don't ignore this. I promise you'll find something you are glad you caught before running your card sort.

- **Think about how you will analyze all the data you collect.** Do that now, before you collect more than you can handle!

- **Don't stop working hard during the sort.** If you are running an in-person card sort, listen to all the discussions, write notes, and make sure you record your results right away.

- **Monitor the card sort.** If you are running a software-based sort, you can relax for a few moments, but don't forget to monitor the progress of the sort as it runs.

Case Study: The Importance of Planning

Leo Frishberg (leo.frishberg@exgate.tek.com)

I was working with a creative agency for an auto manufacturer. A great deal of our work was web related, including reorganizing the web information architecture (content, structure, navigation).

I proposed that we perform a series of card sorts to understand the relationship of the content we had been maintaining. The client project manager was convinced she knew the correct taxonomy and was resistant to user-centered approaches.

So I suggested a "guerrilla" approach to card sorting. The client had its annual convention coming up, the theme for which revolved around games. I proposed that we set up a table where two "contestants" could "compete" by sorting their pile of 75 cards into discrete piles that made sense to them. Although speed wasn't the only criteria for "winning," it was implied that doing it quickly would improve the contestants' odds.

Hundreds of attendees were expected, and I had high hopes of getting substantial participation. (The party was held three separate nights for three separate crowds, giving us even greater possibilities of segmentation.)

For one reason or another, I was not allowed to attend the actual event. What ended up happening was a comedy of errors.

1. The individual who had to perform the card sort was neither well trained, nor well skilled in working with human subjects.

2. She was not prepared for the insanity of doing this activity in the context of a hospitality suite.

3. She was not capable of implementing techniques for capturing the raw data quickly.

Although she did get about 12 participants (about one-third of the numbers I expected), she left all of the data in the hotel room when she exited the affair.

In spite of this particular disaster, I still believe this approach to finding users (at their convention) is a creative way to work around (or with) unwilling project managers.

Use Exploratory Analysis

S o your card sort was a success and now you have a great big bundle of data. You might have a file from an online sorting tool, a set of participants' cards and labels, or a quickly scribbled list of the groups and cards from each session. But how do you figure out what you learned? It's time to get into analysis.

There are two types of analysis: exploratory and statistical. Both approaches aim to help you spot the key patterns in your data and derive useful insights for your project. This chapter focuses on exploratory analysis. This type of analysis is about playing with your data to pick up some quick lessons and new perspectives. Exploratory analysis is fun and easy. It actually encourages you to dig around and find patterns and easy insights you can use right away.

The type of exploratory analysis I outline in this chapter helps you to examine:

- What groups people form.

- What classification schemes people use.

- What content is placed in each group.

- Where individual cards are placed.

- What words people use to describe their groups.

Goals and Exploratory Analysis

Analysis must support your goals of the card sort activity. When planning for analysis, start by looking at your card-sorting goals.

The next sections discuss some of the goals I outlined at the beginning of Chapter 3, "Defining the Need," and how exploratory analysis helps you achieve them.

Learning Broad Ideas

If your goal was to learn broad ideas, you can use either exploratory or statistical analysis (or both). If you only have a small amount of data, stick to exploratory analysis—statistical analysis is probably overkill. If you have a lot of data, start with exploratory analysis and move to statistical if you feel it will help you gain insights.

Determining Whether You're on Track

With a goal of determining whether you are on track with a project, exploratory analysis is usually sufficient. It can help you check your assumptions against the responses of the participants.

Investigating an Idea in Detail

If you want to investigate something in a fair amount of detail, you can use exploratory analysis, but you will need to make sure you spend enough time on it to dig deep.

My Examples

In this and the next chapter, I use two example card sorts to illustrate the analysis process and the types of issues that arise.

The first is for the Information Architecture Summit. For this card sort, I used titles of presentations from three years of the conference. My goal was to learn how people thought about this content, identify potential organization schemes, and, for each organization scheme, determine the main groups that were formed. The card sort contained 99 cards and 19 participants, and the data was originally collected remotely with a range of software tools.

The second is a card sort I run when I teach information architecture workshops. The idea is that the workshop participants are designing a website for a wine region. The content features examples of information that might be included in that type of website—lists of wineries, lists of accommodations and restaurants, local services, and things to see and do. In this case, the card sort contained 39 cards and was completed by 10 participant teams.

For both card sorts, I put the data into my own analysis spreadsheet[1] and statistical software XLSTAT[2] for analysis.

The data for each is available from the book's website, so you can play around with it as well.

---

1 www.rosenfeldmedia.com/books/cardsorting/blog/card_sort_analysis_spreadsheet/

2 www.xlstat.com/en/home/

Preparing for Exploratory Analysis

If your card sort is very simple—with a small number of cards and small number of participants—you may not need to do any preparation. You might be able to get away with a photograph of the cards from a session or a quick write-up of the results from each participant. See Figures 9.1 and 9.2 for examples.

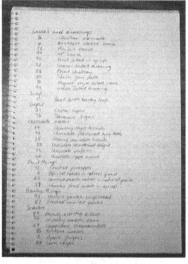

FIGURE 9.1
A finished card sort, complete with labels.

FIGURE 9.2
A written record of the results.

Most of my card sorts are somewhat complex and have many participants. As such, I do most of my exploratory analysis using spreadsheets.

My Analysis Spreadsheet

I have created an Excel spreadsheet that I use for exploratory card-sorting analysis. (The examples in this chapter use it.)

The spreadsheet helps you to record the outcomes, explore your data, and present a summary of the card sort. It manages up to 40 participants and 300 cards. The spreadsheet, plus instructions, is available from the book's website. (See ⋒ www.rosenfeldmedia. com/books/cardsorting/blog/card_sort_analysis_spreadsheet/index.php.)

I recently used the card-sorting spreadsheet template for an exercise with internal employees with one of our channels. It was invaluable when it came time to translate the results to business teams and execs looking to make heads or toes of the data.

—Robert Scrobe (email)

Step 1: Enter Data

Using my analysis spreadsheet, enter your data for each participant. Fill in the card number in the first column and the label of the group they made in the second. A formula automatically pulls in the card name (see Figure 9.3).

	A	B	C	
1	Card no	Group	Card name	
2	9	Activities	Glow-worm caves - tour details, costs and t	D
3	31	Activities	Heritage walk - details of a local walk to see	
4	1	Activities	Sunday arts & crafts market	
5	4	Activities	Historic library - location and opening hours	
6	18	Activities	Winery bus tour - full day	
7	32	Activities	Winery bus tour - half day	
8	13	Events	Application form for the 2007 wine show	
9	22	Events	Winners from the 2006 wine show	
10	3	Events	Annual wine show - date and location	
11	29	Events	Harvest feast - March every year, wineries de	
12	11	Events	Winery walkabout - annual event with special	
13	2	Events	Live music at the pub - schedule of bands	
14	16	Wineries	7th island (vineyard, winery, cellar door) - loc	
15	28	Wineries	Dog leg (winery & cellar door) - location, oper	
16	34	Wineries	Gooda wines (vineyard & cellar door) - openin	

FIGURE 9.3
I list the group and card for each participant.

This will automatically populate a big matrix of all the data—each row represents a card and each column a participant (see Figure 9.4). The row and column intersection has the label for each group. I typically print this out and put it on the wall so I can see everything at once (see Figure 9.5).

	A	B	C	D	E	F
1	Card no	Card name	Sort1		Sort3	Sort4
2	1	Sunday arts & crafts market	Activities	Each participant is represented by a column	Activities	Things to do
3	2	Live music at the pub - schedule of bands	Events	Things to do	Events	Things to do
4	3	Annual wine show - date and location	Events	Vineyards, wines, education & showing	Events	Wine show
5	4	Historic library - location and opening hours	Activities	About the region	Activities	Things to do
6	5	The Local (local pub) - accommodation details, opening hours, m	Accommodation	When you're here	Ac	& drink
7	6	Batterin restaura hours, m	Food	When you're here	E	& drink
8	7	The Pres producer product list	Local products	When you're here	Eating and drinking	Food & drink
9	8	Wine tasting classes (2 hours a week for 6 weeks) - times, costs, details	About wine	Vineyards, wines, education & showing	Activities	Things to do
10	9	Glow-worm caves - tour details, costs and times	Activities	Things to do	Activities	Things to do

Callout: The first two columns show card number and name

Callout: The intersection of row and column shows the group label

FIGURE 9.4
A big worksheet with all the raw data.

FIGURE 9.5
The results, printed and stuck together.

Step 2: Standardize Labels

Participants often use very similar, but not identical, words to create group labels. This makes analysis tricky—it is hard to see any patterns when there are tiny differences getting in the way. To make this process easier and more meaningful, you need to create a set of consistent labels that enables the spreadsheet to group very similar things together more easily.

To do this, create a list of all the categories that participants used. Look at the words people have used for labels and whenever you find labels that are very similar, either in language or idea, create a standardized label. Don't combine them unless the word or the idea is very similar, or you will start combining results that don't belong together. When choosing the term for the standardized label, use the one that has been used by most participants or that represents the idea most clearly.

An example from the winery card sort is in Table 9.1. This shows the most common term, some variants, and the standardized term I used.

TABLE 9.1 STANDARDIZE TERMS

Most Common Term	Variants	Standardized Term
About the region	About region The region	About the region
About wine	About wines About the wine	About wine
Accommodation	Places to stay Sleeping	Accommodation
Events	Wine events Annual events	Events
Eating and drinking	Eating and drinking Food and drink	Eating and drinking

Continue until you have a standardized label for every group. In many card sorts, participants may have created hierarchical groups. Although these are interesting for your analysis, at this step it is easier if you have a flat hierarchy. As you go through the process of standardizing labels, get rid of the hierarchies—use either the broad or detailed labels depending on which fits your cards best.

Use these labels for the analysis steps. (Make sure you keep a copy of the original labels used by participants as well, in case you want to check the original data.)

This will populate another big matrix, which you may also like to print, as shown in Figure 9.6

	A	B	C	D	E	F
1	Card no	Card name	Sort1	Sort2	Sort3	Sort4
2	1	Sunday arts & crafts market	Things to do	Things to do	Things to do	Things to do
3	2	Live music at the pub - schedule of bands	Events	Things to do	Events	Things to do
4	3	Annual wine show - date and location	Events	Vineyards, wines, education & showing	Events	Wine show
5	4	Historic library - location and opening hours	Things to do	About the region	Things to do	Things to do
6	5	The Local (local pub) - accommodation details, opening hours, menu	Accommodation	When you're here	Accommodation	Food & drink
7	6	Battering Ram (takeaway restaurant) - location, opening hours, menu	Food	When you're here	Food & drink	Food & drink
8	7	The Press (local olive grower & producer) - location, opening hours, product list	Local produce	When you're here	Food & drink	Food & drink
9	8	Wine tasting classes (2 hours a week for 6 weeks) - times, costs, details	About wine	Vineyards, wines, education & showing	Things to do	Things to do
10	9	Glow-worm caves - tour details, costs and times	Things to do	Things to do	Things to do	Things to do
11	10	Cottage comforts (bed & breakfast) - costs, location, booking details	Accommodation	When you're here	Accommodation	Accommodation

FIGURE 9.6

The wine region card sort matrix showing the standardized labels.

It will also populate a sheet that shows how often a card was placed in each category (this, too, is handy to print), as shown in Figure 9.7.

	A	B	C	D	E	F	G	H	I
1	Card no	Card name	About the region	Things to do	Accommodation	Wineries	About wine	Eating	Events
2	1	Sunday arts & crafts market		90%					10%
3	2	Live music at the pub - schedule of bands		70%					30%
4	3	Annual wine show - date and location							30%
5	4	Historic library - location and opening hours	30%	70%					
6	5	The Local (local pub) - accommodation details, c			30%			10%	
7	6	Battering Ram (takeaway restaurant) - location,						40%	
8	7	The Press (local olive grower & producer) - locat		30%					
9	8	Wine tasting classes (2 hours a week for 6 week		30%			20%		
10	9	Glow-worm caves - tour details, costs and times		100%					
11	10	Cottage comforts (bed & breakfast) - costs, loc			90%				
12	11	Winery walkabout - annual event with special ta		20%					40%
13	12	Weather through the year	100%						
14	13	Application form for the 2007 wine show							20%
15	14	Winter in the vineyard - things that happen in th	10%			30%			20%
16	15	Hilton hotel - package deals, location, costs, bo			90%				
17	16	7th island (vineyard, winery, cellar door) - locati				60%			
18	17	Marlowes (vineyard & restaurant) - location, ope				40%		10%	
19	18	Winery bus tour - full day		60%					
20	19	Map of the region	100%						
21	20	The Vintner's palace (microbrewery) - location,				10%		20%	
22	21	Wine tasting classes (short - 3 hour session) - t		30%			20%		
23	22	Winners from the 2006 wine show							20%
24	23	List of services from local businesses (hairdresse	40%	10%					
25	24	History of the region	100%						
26	25	Drinking the menu (wine bar) - location, opening						20%	

FIGURE 9.7

The analysis spreadsheet generates another sheet—this one shows how often a card was placed in a category.

Start the Analysis

Your detailed analysis should encompass all the different areas that
you are exploring, including analyzing groups, card placement, labels,
organizational schemes, how accurately people have grouped content,
participant comments, and the closed card sort. We'll look at all these areas.

Analyze Groups

First, start with the groups that your participants have created, as this will lead
you to figure out how they think and categorize. I've broken this into two steps.

Step 1: Examine the Groups Your Participants Created

Because one of the main uses of card sorting is to determine what groups
exist in a set of content, the main part of exploratory analysis is to look at
the groups that people created.

This is where it can be very handy to have the big matrix (see Figure 9.7)
printed out and stuck to the wall—it helps you see everything at once.
When looking at this, take note of the following details:

- The actual groups people created.

- Whether everyone did a similar thing, or whether the results were
  wildly different.

- What confirmed your expectations.

- If there are any surprises.

As an example of the types of things you might spot, my analysis of data
from the IA Summit card sort showed the following:

- There were many more groups than I expected, and they were very
  diverse. I hadn't realized there were so many ways that content could
  be grouped.

- Some participants had created quirky labels that I would need to
  dig into. (For example, Nuts and Bolts could mean more than one
  thing, Metatags for All Seasons was intriguing, I hadn't a clue what
  Boundaries meant, and what on earth is IA for You!)

- There were quite a few combined groups (such as Taxonomy, Tags, and Classification) that I'd also have to look at more deeply.

- I was also surprised that a lot of people created a group called Case Studies—such a large proportion of the content is in case studies that I didn't think people would use it as a group.

At this step, you are likely to spot all sorts of things you find interesting and want to follow up on later. Make a note of them as you go.

Step 2: Start Deeper Analysis of Groups

Now that you have a good idea of the groups that people created and a set of standard labels, it is time to explore the data in some depth.

Start by identifying groups that were used consistently by participants. Look at each group that participants created and note which cards they included in it (see Figure 9.8).

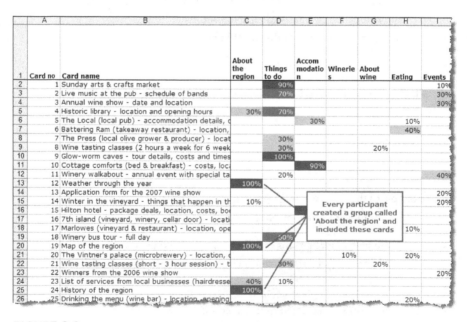

	A	B	C	D	E	F	G	H	I
1	Card no	Card name	About the region	Things to do	Accommodation	Wineries	About wine	Eating	Events
2	1	Sunday arts & crafts market		90%					10%
3	2	Live music at the pub - schedule of bands		70%					30%
4	3	Annual wine show - date and location							30%
5	4	Historic library - location and opening hours	30%	70%					
6	5	The Local (local pub) - accommodation details, c			30%			10%	
7	6	Battering Ram (takeaway restaurant) - location,						40%	
8	7	The Press (local olive grower & producer) - locat		30%					
9	8	Wine tasting classes (2 hours a week for 6 week		30%			20%		
10	9	Glow-worm caves - tour details, costs and times		100%					
11	10	Cottage comforts (bed & breakfast) - costs, loc;			90%				
12	11	Winery walkabout - annual event with special ta		20%					40%
13	12	Weather through the year	100%						
14	13	Application form for the 2007 wine show							20%
15	14	Winter in the vineyard - things that happen in th	10%						20%
16	15	Hilton hotel - package deals, location, costs, bo							
17	16	7th island (vineyard, winery, cellar door) - locati							
18	17	Marlowes (vineyard & restaurant) - location, ope						10%	
19	18	Winery bus tour - full day		50%					
20	19	Map of the region	100%						
21	20	The Vintner's palace (microbrewery) - location, c				10%		20%	
22	21	Wine tasting classes (short - 3 hour session) - t		30%			20%		
23	22	Winners from the 2006 wine show							20%
24	23	List of services from local businesses (hairdresse	40%	10%					
25	24	History of the region	100%						
26	25	Drinking the menu (wine bar) - location, opening						20%	

Every participant created a group called 'About the region' and included these cards

FIGURE 9.8

In the wine region sort everyone created a category called About the Region with some very consistent cards.

Mostly, when participants create similar groups, they will contain similar cards. This is great because this type of group usually represents an idea that everyone understands and means they have similar expectations. For example, in card sorts on corporate sites, I almost always find a group called About Us that has a consistent set of cards.

Sometimes participants will create similarly labeled groups but include quite different cards. This happened with the IA Summit card sort. Eighteen participants created a group called Case Studies or something similar. (I was the only person who didn't, which I thought was especially interesting.) When I looked more deeply at this group, I found that cards included were very diverse—a few cards were almost always in the group, but out of the 99 cards in the sort, more than half were put into that group by at least one participant. This was very interesting, so I dug deeper. The cards placed consistently were those that had the words "case study" in their titles, or had a title that clearly indicated it was a real-world example of a project. The cards that were put in that group least frequently were all ones that didn't fit strongly anywhere else. The remainder of the cards depended on the participant's other groups—sometimes they fit better with other groups, sometimes not. See Figure 9.9.

	A	B	C	D	E	F	G	H
1	Card no	Card name	Case studies	Classification	Methods	Interaction design	General IA	Content management
2	1	The aesthetic imperative: Four perspectives on		5%		26%	5%	
3	2	Taxonomies, controlled vocabularies, and ontolog		37%	5%			
4	3	Using facet analysis for improving information ac	16%	21%				
5	4	Creating no-duh deliverables	5%		16%		5%	
6	5	Creating a consistent enterprise web navigation	5%		11%		11%	
7	6	XIA: Xtreme IA			16%		21%	
8	7	Redesigning a digital video digital library	79%		5%	5%		
9	8	Making personas more powerful		32%		5%		
10	9	Emerging content requirements for news product	11%			5%		53%
11	10	Information search experience: Emotions in infor			5%	11%	5%	
12	11	Blind leading the blind: Theorizing a web for the	16%			5%	11%	
13	12	Rapid user mental modelling at ebay: A case stu	79%		5%			
14	13	4 myths about taxonomies & dublin core: Exampl	26%	37%				
15	14	Information visualisation: Failed experiment or fu	11%		5%	5%	11%	
16	15	Architecting time: Designing online events and o	16%		11%	32%	11%	
17	16	Fun with faceted browsing		26%	5%	11%		
18	17	An ethnographic study of how stockbrokers use	63%		5%			
19	18	Recycle, reuse, and rebuild: Information architec	11%		26%		11%	

FIGURE 9.9
The IA Summit card sort showing how diverse the Case Studies group was.

While you are looking at cards in each group, make sure you have a good look at the Other, Miscellaneous, and Don't Know groups (most sorts have them). These groups can help you to understand content that was poorly labeled, that participants didn't understand, or that just didn't fit anywhere.

After you have finished looking at the groups to see what was similar, do the same and see what was different. For most of my card sorts, this process is the most useful. Differences usually provide much better insights than similarities.

Analyze Card Placement

Another way of looking at the data is to examine each card and see what groups it was assigned to. The analysis process is a bit different than the previous steps. Here it is less important to look for consistency—you have done that when looking at the groups. Looking at each card gives you an idea of what participants think a card means.

Again, the example shown in Figure 9.10 will help.

	A	B	C	D	E	F	G	
1	Card no	Card name	Sort1	Sort2	Sort3	Sort4	Sort5	So
2	1	The aesthetic imperative: Four perspectives on aesthetics to impact the user experience.	Emotion & aesthetics	Nuts and Bolts	Interaction design	Emotion and aesthetics	User Experience Design	1x8 fac
3	2	Taxonomies, controlled vocabularies, and ontologies	CVs & taxonomies	Back to Basics	Taxonomy, tags and classification	Metadata	Organizing, Relating & Finding	Cla CV
4	3	Using facet analysis for improving information access to marginalized communities	Facets	Global Issues	Taxonomy, tags and classification	Facets	Case Studies	Fac
5	4	Creating no-duh deliverables	Communicatio n	The Business of IA	IA: Presentation and output	Deliverables	Communicatin g	De
6	5	Creating a consistent enterprise web navigation solution	Enterprise IA	Nuts and Bolts	IA: Creating the architecture	Enterprise IA	Enterprise IA	Ent
7	6	XIA: Xtreme IA	Odd bits	Future Directions	Discussions	Methods	Methods & Techniques	IA
8	7	Redesigning a digital video digital library	IA foundations	Case Studies: Real World Examples	Cases and studies	Case studies	Case Studies	1x0 fac
9	8	Making personas more powerful	User research	User Centered Design Issues	Interaction design	Deliverables	Methods & Techniques	IA Me
10	9	Emerging content requirements for news products	Odd bits	Content Concerns	Content management	Content management	Case Studies	1x0 fac

FIGURE 9.10

Examining each card and the groups it was in.

For example, participants put the card labeled Making Personas More Powerful into these groups:

- User research (twice)

- User centered design issues

- Interaction design

- Deliverables (twice)

- Methods and techniques

- IA methodologies

- Design tools: research and innovation

- Learning from the user

- IA basics

- Fundamentals

- Usability methods

- Techniques (twice)

- Practical: tools and methods for IAs

- Development/testing

- Usability

- IA fundamentals

Even this simple example is interesting. Clearly, some people think of personas as having to do with users (a topic), some as a method (something you do), and some as a deliverable (an end result).

I may not do anything explicitly with that information, but it helps inform me as to how my users think about a topic.

Don't over-analyze this, though. It only tells you a small amount about how the users think—given that most people will have put the card in one group only, it doesn't tell us whether an individual participant might think personas are about users, a method, and a deliverable all at once.

Analyze Labels

While you are looking at groups, it's important to pay particular attention to the way they have been labeled. For each group, look at what they called it. Pay attention to:

- **Similarities in terminology.** For a particular idea, see how similar the label was. For example, I think About the Region, The Region, and About Region all represent the same idea, and I'd feel comfortable using any as a navigation label.

- **Differences in terminology.** However, Things to Do and Attractions and Activities are quite different words that still represent a fairly clear concept. You could probably use either of them in navigation and people would understand what the category was about. I'd choose the one that works best with other category labels.

- **Formality of language.** Sometimes, people will use very precise language (Dining, Restaurants) and sometimes informal (Places to Eat). Very different label types may tell you something about the way your audience uses language.

Analyze Organizational Schemes

A more general trend to look for is whether people have created groups according to a particular organization scheme.

For example, on a movie site, people may organize the cards by genre, director, or year. On intranet projects, some participants sort the cards according to audience, others according to task, and most by topic.

Most often, you won't see a consistent scheme, but a strange mixture of schemes or a simple grouping by topic. At the end of the sort, I like to ask participants whether they have used an underlying method—they may be able to explain it to you, or may not have used one at all.

Analyze How Accurately Participants
Have Grouped Content

I also like to look at how accurately participants have grouped the cards. I know that I said before that there are no wrong answers. Well, that's true, but most content has some type of internal correctness, and it is interesting to examine how close participants come to that correctness.

For the IA Summit card sort, many of the cards that ended up in a group called Case Study or something similar actually weren't case studies at all. A case study is a concrete example about a particular situation, not a presentation about theory or about a new idea or approach. I thought this was quite interesting because it told me that titles didn't communicate the type of presentation (well, I knew that, but this confirmed it), that Case Study was perhaps a looser concept for the participants than it was for me, and that it was possibly being used as an Other category.

In a recent intranet card sort, I noticed that some participants organized the cards according to who was responsible for it, but placed some cards in the "wrong" group. This indicated to me that some of the content didn't fit neatly in the organization (something that was supported by other research) and that participants really weren't sure who was responsible for some things.[3]

But be careful with how you interpret accuracy. While you may have found that the technically correct structure has some flaws, there may be other reasons that people are inaccurate. You may not have labeled the content clearly, or participants may not have understood the content well or may not have been very careful during the card sort.

On a related topic, sometimes you'll spot something that just seems wrong—something that is out of step with everything else that a participant has done. This can happen—people can make mistakes during the activity, the facilitator may transcribe something incorrectly, or you may accidentally jumble some cards. When I was analyzing the IA Summit card sort, I found two strange placements in the data from my own sort, and I think I must

---

3   By the way, it is usually not a good idea to organize an intranet (or a website for that matter) according to the organizational chart, but that doesn't mean people won't do it in the card sort.

have dropped cards into the wrong category in the software tool. If you are sure there is a mistake, don't hesitate to fix it—it is better to do the analysis without obvious errors in the data.

Analyze Participant Comments

Don't forget to analyze the other data that you may collect during the card sort—for example, any notes that you have made, as well as the participant comments. I usually try to capture general comments that participants make when working in teams, information on which cards were put together first and which were left until the end, and any interesting spatial patterns (for more detail of things to collect see Chapter 4, "Choose the Method"). I also make sure I capture the exact words that people use, as this phrasing can be another potential source of ideas for groups and labels.

I often find that the participant comments provide some of the best insights into reasons people create particular types of groupings and how they think. It is important not to lose this when you start to analyze the data. It is easy to get so drawn into data that the comments go unanalyzed.

Analyze a Closed Card Sort

Closed card sorts are much simpler to analyze than open sorts. I document the result with a big spreadsheet—categories in the top row and cards in the first column (see Figure 9.11). Then I simply count how many times each participant placed a card in a particular category.

Card no	Card name	Accessibility	Commun ication	Content manage ment	Delivera bles	IA Foundations	IA and business
28	Information architecture and alzheimer's	5					
11	Blind leading the blind: Theorizing a web	5					
47	Change, influence and IA at the BBC						3
76	Innovation vs. Best practice conflict or op						
54	A foray across boundaries: Applying IA t						5
82	Game changing: How you can transform		4				
57	Talking the talk: Helping IAs speak the l		2				3
63	Leading a team of IAs: The manager's pe						5
94	Selling IA: Getting execs to say yes		2				3
30	Evangelism 101		2			1	
35	Implementing a pattern library in the real		1			1	
64	Faceted classification in the government						
7	Redesigning a digital video digital library						
36	To hold or to access: Building IA of the d						
21	Stories from the field: Never consider yo		1				
12	Rapid user mental modelling at ebay: A						
19	Rebuilding trust in user centred design,					1	
40	Applying IA to community: A case study						
25	Design and communication: Other ways		5				

FIGURE 9.11
Analyzing a closed card sort—categories are across the top and cards
are down the side.

When you're analyzing, look at the following information:

- Differences between what you thought would happen and what
  participants actually did. Sometimes you'll have a clear idea about
  where you thought content should go and participants will do
  something quite different.

- Determine if the content is evenly distributed between categories or
  clumped in a few. If it is clumped, those categories may be too broad
  for your content, and you may want to break them down (or you may
  just have provided more content for those than others).

- Check any content that is placed in a number of categories. If you have
  a lot of content like this, your categories may overlap too much, or your
  content may not be clearly defined.

Chapter 9 Summary/Tips

If running the card sort was the fun part, analysis is the painful part, at least until you get going. Exploratory analysis is like playing around in the data—looking for connections that make you think "hey, that's interesting" or that show patterns of behavior. You can use exploratory analysis for most card sorts, unless you collect too much data, and then it's better to use statistical analysis, covered in Chapter 10, "Use Statistical Analysis."

When doing exploratory analysis, look for:

- What groups were created.

- Where cards were placed.

- What people used for group labels.

- What organizational scheme people used.

- Whether people created accurate or inaccurate groups.

And don't forget to analyze the participants' comments if you have them.

CHAPTER 10

Use Statistical
Analysis

S tatistical analysis is about using a range of statistical algorithms to highlight patterns in data. Statistical methods are particularly useful when you have a lot of data to analyze.

Statistical analysis helps you:

- Determine whether there are consistent patterns in your data.

- Identify the most consistent patterns.

- Compare results from different groups of people.

While statistical analysis is powerful, there are plenty of traps to watch out for. You have to understand the statistics, you have to be careful not to get drawn into the easy result, and you still need to use exploratory methods as well.

Goals and Statistical Analysis

If you are considering using statistical analysis, think about whether it will help you achieve your goal from card sorting. Looking at some of the goals I outlined at the beginning of Chapter 3, "Defining the Need," you'll see that statistical analysis may help in these situations.

Learning Broad Ideas

If your goal was to learn broad ideas, you can use either exploratory or statistical analysis (or both). If you have a lot of data, start with exploratory analysis and move to statistical if you feel it will help you gain insights.

Investigating an Idea in Detail

If you want to investigate something in a fair amount of detail, statistical analysis may help you see key patterns that you can use to follow up with more statistics or more exploratory analysis.

Comparing People

Statistical analysis is particularly strong when identifying differences between different groups of participants. This area can sometimes be harder to spot with exploratory analysis, although it will help you identify reasons for differences.

Justifying a Recommendation

The analysis method you choose for this goal will depend on the organizational context and whom you need to communicate with—think very carefully about your audience and how they will react to your analysis. For example, if you are working in an organization with many scientists, statistical analysis may be convincing, or you could get yourself in trouble if they question your methods.

Analyzing the Data

There is an endless array of statistical methods that can be used to analyze card-sorting data.[1] Rather than go through them all, I'm going to outline three that I use most often and that are available in many statistical analysis tools. The three methods that I use are:

- **K-means cluster analysis:** The analysts choose how many groups they want to see and the statistics find the best group.

- **Hierarchical cluster analysis (HCA):** The statistics create a hierarchy that best fits the data relationships.

- **Multidimensional scaling (MDS):** This provides a visual representation of "closeness" of data.

I use these three because they are conceptually suitable for card sorting, have underlying ideas that are fairly easy to understand, are widely available in statistical software, and produce outputs that can be presented visually.

Statistical Analysis Challenges

The main challenge for statistical analysis is that you actually need to know your statistics. No statistical technique is straightforward—all have many variables (also called *control parameters*) to choose from and you need to know enough to choose the right ones.

---

1   The most comprehensive reference I know is Coxon, A. M. (1999). *Sorting Data: Collection and Analysis*. Sage University Papers Series on Quantitative Applications in the Social Sciences, 07-127. Thousand Oaks, CA: Sage.

You also need to know enough about how the analysis works to interpret the results properly. I have explained some of the issues in the discussion about each method in the following sections, but it is beyond the scope of this book to explain every option in depth.

> *The choice of control parameters in both cases is crucial to the quality and meaningfulness of the results, and the understanding of those parameters is not easily attained. Whilst software may increase the visibility of the parameters, it will generally not assist the analyst in making appropriate choices.*
>
> —Steve Baty, Meld Consulting (http://meld.com.au/)

Another challenge is that statistical techniques can produce such nice outputs that it is easy to get drawn into a simple answer and forget about the underlying reason for the output. I have seen many cases where analysts used statistics to provide the *one true answer* and didn't attempt to understand the underlying issues. To get the best out of statistical methods, try a few different types and use different variables within one type. Look for similarities and differences between each. As with exploratory analysis, any similarities you find represent concepts that are consistent; differences give you opportunity to consider and explore.

Statistical methods do not give you everything you need for a project:

- While they can help you spot patterns, they don't allow you to identify why a pattern exists.

- Statistical analysis focuses on finding the most consistent patterns. But for an IA project, the inconsistencies offer some of the most useful insights.

- Statistical analysis methods combine results from all users, and may not represent what any individual person did.

The last trap is that statistical software tools can be hard to access. The more powerful ones are very expensive—as an independent practitioner, they've always been beyond my reach. And the default statistical tools provided by some card-sorting software programs may not be good enough. They do not give you the ability to choose your statistical method, and may not use the most appropriate statistical algorithms.

I've been using an Excel plug-in called XLSTAT.[2] It caters to the analysis methods I outline in this chapter, uses sensible defaults, and has a wide enough range of variables for those who know how to use them. It also creates better pictures of the results than I've seen from some of the expensive statistical tools. It is not free, but it is within my price range.

Preparing for Statistical Analysis

How you prepare data for statistical analysis will vary depending on the statistical tool you use—each has its own input format. Some may allow you to import data from a spreadsheet, whereas some may need data to be keyed straight into the tool. I can offer little guidance on this, as the tools vary so much.

Here are some tips that apply to most tools:

- If participants have created groups labeled Other, Miscellaneous, and Don't Know (or similar titles), for example, make each card a separate group. They are not a real conceptual group, and cards should not lumped together.

- If you have used long titles on your cards, you may need to create short titles for them—statistical tools that produce a visual representation of the data can be impossible to read if the titles are long.

- If participants created hierarchical groups, flatten them into a single level—either aggregate up to a broader group or split them into smaller groups. Most statistical techniques don't work with hierarchies.

- If participants have discarded cards, determine whether your statistical software allows discards (many won't).

---

2 XLSTAT: www.xlstat.com/

- If you let participants include a card in more than one place, choose one best location. Most statistical software doesn't work with duplicate cards.

- If you have different participant groups (business and personal consumers, or different demographic groups), analyze each group separately to compare results.

- Similarly, if participants used different organization approaches (movies by genre or year), separate those and analyze each on its own. The results will be misleading if they are combined.

Method 1: K-Means Cluster Analysis

In K-Means cluster analysis, the analyst chooses how many groups (clusters) should be formed and the tool determines the best way to split cards into that number of groups. It is a particularly useful method for exploring different ways data can be grouped and for determining group boundaries.

K-Means is one of the simplest forms of cluster analysis. It works by first assigning objects randomly to the set number of categories and then calculating the center of each category. It then moves objects between the categories, calculates how similar the objects in each category are, and continues to move objects until a suitable level of similarity has been reached.

One of the key aspects of K-Means analysis is that the initial assignment of objects to a category will affect the final output. Each time you run the analysis, you may get a different result—this is a disadvantage if you are looking for a clear outcome. It is also problematic if you are trying to compare types of people because it is hard to know whether differences are caused by the starting cluster or because of a real difference between people.

It is, however, a great way to explore possible groupings. By running the process a number of times, you can see how the results vary. Figures 10.1 and 10.2 show typical K-Means analysis output.

	A	B	C
1	k-means, 7 clusters, first run	k-means, 7 clusters, second run	k-means, 7 clusters, third run
2	Sunday arts & crafts market	Sunday arts & crafts market	Sunday arts & crafts market
3	Live music at the pub	Live music at the pub	Live music at the pub
4	Historic library	Historic library	Historic library
5	Glow-worm caves	Glow-worm caves	GlowWorm
6	Heritage walk	Heritage walk	Heritage walk
7		Wine tasting classes - long course	
8		Wine tasting classes - short course	
9	Annual wine show	Annual wine show	Annual wine show
10	Application form for the 2007 wine show	Application form for the 2007 wine show	Application form for the 2007 wine show
11	Winners from the 2006 wine show	Winners from the 2006 wine show	Winners from the 2006 wine show
12	Winery bus tour - full day	Winery bus tour - full day	Winery bus tour - full day
13	Winery bus tour - half day	Winery bus tour - half day	Winery bus tour - half day
14	Wine tasting classes - long course	7th island (vineyard, winery, cellar door)	Wine tasting classes - long course
15	Wine tasting classes - short course	Dog leg (winery & cellar door)	Wine tasting classes - short course
16	7th island (vineyard, winery, cellar door)	Gooda wines (vineyard & cellar door)	7th island (vineyard, winery, cellar door)
17	Dog leg (winery & cellar door)		Marlowes
18	Gooda wines (vineyard & cellar door)		Dog leg (winery & cellar door)
19			Gooda wines (vineyard & cellar door)
20	The Local (local pub)	The Local (local pub)	The Local (local pub)
21	Battering Ram (takeaway restaurant)	Battering Ram (takeaway restaurant)	Battering Ram (takeaway restaurant)
22	The Press (local olive grower & producer)	The Press (local olive grower & producer)	The Press (local olive grower & producer)
23	The Vintner's palace (microbrewery)	The Vintner's palace (microbrewery)	The Vintner's palace (microbrewery)
24	Drinking the menu (wine bar)	Drinking the menu (wine bar)	Drinking the menu (wine bar)
25	Beez neez (honey producer)	Beez neez (honey producer)	Beez neez (honey producer)
26	The wining wife (restaurant)	The wining wife (restaurant)	The wining wife (restaurant)
27	Cottage comforts (bed & breakfast)	Winery walkabout	Harvest feast
28	Hilton hotel	Harvest feast	About sauvignon blanc
29	Winery walkabout	Cottage comforts (bed & breakfast)	About pinot

FIGURE 10.1

K-Means analysis output using seven clusters each time—note the different results.

When I use K-Means, I run the analysis a few times for a particular number of clusters and then again with different cluster sizes. (To get an idea of what cluster sizes to use, I look at the raw data to identify minimum, maximum, and most common number of groups created by participants.)

	A	B	C
1	k-means, 5 clusters	k-means, 7 clusters	k-means, 10 clusters
2	7th island (vineyard, winery, cellar door)	7th island (vineyard, winery, cellar door)	7th island (vineyard, winery, cellar door)
3	Dog leg (winery & cellar door)	Dog leg (winery & cellar door)	Dog leg (winery & cellar door)
4	Gooda wines (vineyard & cellar door)	Gooda wines (vineyard & cellar door)	Gooda wines (vineyard & cellar door)
5	Marlowes (vineyard & restaurant)	Marlowes (vineyard & restaurant)	Marlowes (vineyard & restaurant)
6	Battering Ram (takeaway restaurant)	Battering Ram (takeaway restaurant)	Battering Ram (takeaway restaurant)
7	Drinking the menu (wine bar)	Drinking the menu (wine bar)	Drinking the menu (wine bar)
8	The Local (local pub)	The Local (local pub)	The Local (local pub)
9	The Vintner's palace (microbrewery)	The Vintner's palace (microbrewery)	The Vintner's palace (microbrewery)
10	The wining wife (restaurant)	The wining wife (restaurant)	The wining wife (restaurant)
11		The Press (local olive grower & producer)	The Press (local olive grower & producer)
12		Beez neez (honey producer)	Beez neez (honey producer)
13	About pinot	About pinot	About pinot
14	About sauvignon blanc	About sauvignon blanc	About sauvignon blanc
15	Winter in the vineyard	Winter in the vineyard	Winter in the vineyard
16	Annual wine show	Annual wine show	Annual wine show
17	Application form for the 2007 wine show	Application form for the 2007 wine show	Application form for the 2007 wine show
18	Winners from the 2006 wine show	Winners from the 2006 wine show	Winners from the 2006 wine show
19		Harvest feast	Harvest feast
20		Winery walkabout	Winery walkabout
21	History of the region	History of the region	History of the region
22	Map of the region	Map of the region	Map of the region
23	Weather - 3 day forecast	Weather - 3 day forecast	Weather - 3 day forecast
24	Weather through the year	Weather through the year	Weather through the year
25	Tourist bureau	Tourist bureau	List of services from local businesses
26	List of services from local businesses	List of services from local businesses	Tourist bureau

FIGURE 10.2

K-Means analysis output using three different cluster sizes.

In the output, I often look for the number of clusters that allows me to label them sensibly. For example, a small number of broad clusters are hard to name, which tells me they are not yet coherent groups, so I keep making finer clusters until I can spot concepts that can be labeled.

The main danger with K-Means analysis is that it is very tempting to say "I have six top level navigation items—what should go in them?" Please don't do this—use the technique to explore, not to give you an oversimplified answer.

Method 2: Hierarchical Cluster Analysis

If you have used a card-sorting tool in the past, you may have come across hierarchical cluster analysis (HCA)—it was the only output from the first dedicated card-sorting software tool, and some tools still offer it as a primary output.

HCA and K-Means are similar in that they are both clustering methods, but HCA is different from K-Means in that it does not assign cards to groups—it builds a hierarchy made of clusters of cards.

An HCA starts with the software making a calculation of the distance between each pair of objects (cards). Then pairs of cards placed in a group by lots of participants have a low distance score (they are close together), and cards placed in a group infrequently have a high distance score (they are farther apart). There are many, many ways to calculate the distance between cards—the software I use has more than 40 methods. One of the most commonly used is Euclidean distance, and if you don't want to learn all the methods, this one will do fine.

With the initial distance calculation, the software combines the closest two cards into a cluster and recalculates the distance measure again (using the cluster as one object). It then creates a cluster from the next closest pair, recalculates the distance measure, and so on until all cards have been included.

There are different methods for calculating the distance between clusters. Three of the most common are the following:

- **Single linkage.** The distance between two clusters is calculated as the distance of the two closest objects. Single linkage can give very long clusters that look like they are built up object by object, and it can be difficult to see the clusters (see Figure 10.3).

- **Complete linkage.** The distance between two clusters is determined by the greatest distance between any two objects in the different clusters. Complete linkage can provide very compact clusters (see Figure 10.4).

- **Average linkage.** The distance between clusters is determined by the average distance between objects in the clusters. This is a good compromise between the previous two methods and may represent the data well (see Figure 10.5).

The result of the calculation is shown as a dendrogram—a hierarchical tree, as shown in Figures 10.3-10.5.

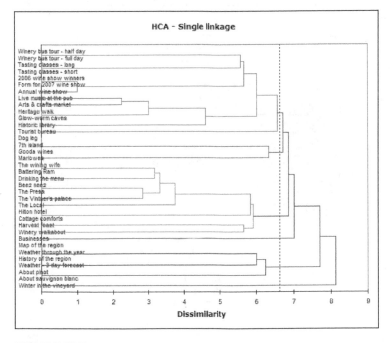

FIGURE 10.3
A single-linkage dendrogram—note how the objects appear to be chained together.

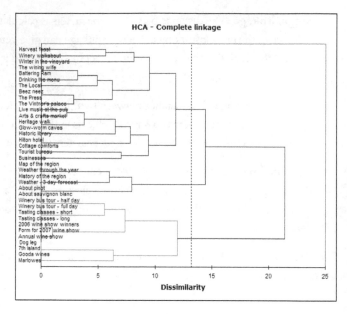

FIGURE 10.4
A complete linkage
dendrogram—note
how the clusters
are more clumped
together than the
single-linkage
diagram.

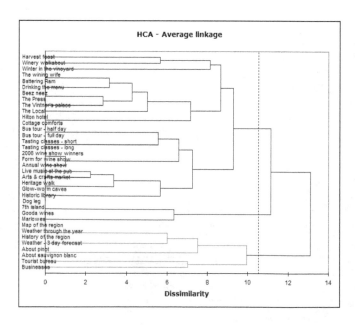

FIGURE 10.5
An average-linking
dendrogram—note
the characteristics
of single and
complete linkage:
some chaining,
some clusters.

To interpret a dendrogram, note that the numbers at the bottom are a calculation of the measure of distance between two items—if there is a vertical bar between two items at 0, the distance is 0 and the two items were placed together by every participant. Everything else is a relative measure of closeness, depending on the type of dendrogram you select (and the numbers are all relative, not absolute—you'll see from the scales that each has calculated different scales).

The best way to use a dendrogram for analysis is, like other methods, to run a number of analyses and compare the outcomes. Look at which cards were clustered together in all analyses, which were always apart, and identify the variations.

Method 3: Multidimensional Scaling

Multidimensional scaling (MDS) is a method that provides a visual representation of the closeness of items. MDS plots objects on a map—objects that are similar to each other are close together, and objects that are different from each other are far away from each other. MDS is usually done in two and three dimensions as they can be plotted and examined by eye.

MDS uses a dissimilarity matrix as input (see Figure 10.6), which is a matrix that calculates a value that represents how dissimilar (or how far apart) two objects are. (HCA can also use a dissimilarity matrix—it depends on your statistical software whether you have to create the matrix or whether it is created in the background.) As with HCA, there are many ways to calculate a dissimilarity matrix and, again, the most common is Euclidean distance.

	Arts	MusicPub	WineShow	Library	TheLocal	BatterR	ThePress	WineClas	GlowWorm
Arts	0	2.236	6.403	4.583	7.483	7.348	9.110	6.782	3.000
MusicPub	2.236	0	6.000	5.099	8.185	7.141	8.832	7.416	3.742
WineShow	6.403	6.000	0	7.483	9.000	7.550	9.899	7.000	7.071
Library	4.583	5.099	7.483	0	9.849	8.185	10.954	8.062	6.481
TheLocal	7.483	8.185	9.000	9.849	0	4.899	5.196	7.616	7.280
BatterR	7.348	7.141	7.550	8.185	4.899	0	4.359	7.874	7.550
ThePress	9.110	8.832	9.899	10.954	5.196	4.359	0	10.909	8.602
WineClas	6.782	7.416	7.000	8.062	7.616	7.874	10.909	0	7.810
GlowWorm	3.000	3.742	7.071	6.481	7.280	7.550	8.602	7.810	0

FIGURE 10.6

Part of a dissimilarity matrix showing the distance between pairs of cards.

There are two types of multidimensional scaling: metric and nonmetric. Metric MDS is used when the data is for measured distances, and is therefore the most appropriate for card-sorting data (as the dissimilarity matrix is a measure of distance between cards).

Unlike the other two techniques I described, no further statistical manipulation happens. The idea behind MDS is that it represents the distances in the dissimilarity matrix as well as possible. Like K-Means analysis, the output is based on where it starts processing the data, and the output will be different each time the analysis is run. Figures 10.7 and 10.8 show the different results of two MDS analyses.

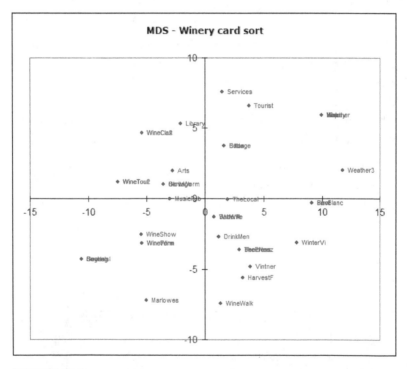

FIGURE 10.7

Output from a two-dimensional multidimensional scaling analysis (overlapping items are cards placed together by all participants).

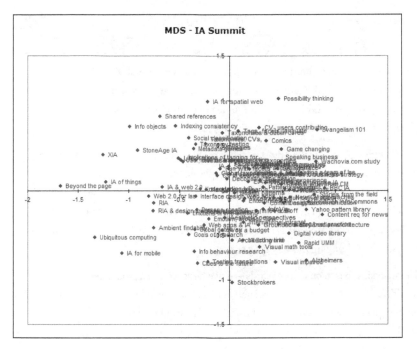

FIGURE 10.8

MDS for the IA Summit data—too much data, long labels, and no consistent pattern made for a messy result. All I can get out of this is an idea of the outliers.

Why I Worry About Cluster Analysis

Although I use statistical techniques as a support to exploratory analysis, I would never use them as the only analysis method. Although the cluster analysis statistics help show some interesting patterns, I think there are some real methodological issues that make me wary of relying on them too heavily for analyzing card-sorting data:

- The underlying statistical method requires people to conduct the sort in a way that is best for the statistics, not best for people. For example, people like to make hierarchies, put cards in more than one place, and discard cards that they don't think are relevant. Cluster analysis is based on the premise of a single level of mutually exclusive groups with all cards present. People have to behave in a way that suits the analysis, thus changing the way they sort.

- The analysis is based on pairs of cards—if two cards were in a group, they are considered to be together and calculated as a pair. But when I observe card sorts, I see how people make groups. They don't think "this card goes with this card, so I'll put them together." They think "this card is about such-and-such; this card is also about such-and-such—I'll put them together." It's subtle, but participants don't think about the pairs of cards, they think about the group of cards. Some groups may have cards that don't relate to one another at all, which is especially true when participants make large, broad groups. This can be managed by asking participants to rank cards according to what fits best, but is a fairly significant extra step for participants.

- The idea behind clustering techniques is to find a single best fit. The result that you may see from cluster analysis is unlikely to reflect any groups formed by an individual. The outcome may not represent any type of real-world result.

These issues are important—cluster analysis focuses on pairs of cards and treats all pairs as statistically equal, even though they may not be equal. I like to use cluster analysis to spot key issues in big datasets, but I get much more out of an exploratory, less statistical, approach.

Chapter 10 Summary/Tips

Statistical analysis is tricky, but it can illuminate trends and connections that you may not have noticed during exploratory analysis. Keep these points in mind about statistical analysis:

- Use statistical analysis only when you actually need it—when you have a lot of data or want to compare audiences.

- Don't rely on one statistical method—try a couple.

- Run each method more than once to find similarities and differences.

Case Study: When Categories Don't Come Together

Donna Spencer

Earlier this year I worked on a website redesign project for a large company. A redesign was needed as the website was organized according to the company structure and most users could not find the information they needed. This was a challenging project for many reasons. The content was of poor quality and poorly structured. The company had a very diverse set of responsibilities, some of them quite technical, and most of them were completely unfamiliar to me. There were internal politics and egos of upper management to cope with (their only concern was "where's my stuff?"). And, of course, the timetable was extremely tight.

My job was to make sure that users could find information, illustrate the company's purpose and areas of expertise, allow the website to expand as the company took on new responsibilities, and make managers happy.

I spent a long time analyzing the content—learning what was on the website, the types of information, topics covered, and the key relationships between topics. Even after staring at the content for days, I couldn't figure out how it fit together or how I could reorganize it. I even started to think it might not fit together—that maybe the company had a strange set of unrelated responsibilities.

So I decided to run a card sort with internal staff. I wanted to see how people who knew the domain would sort the content.

I identified the main topics in content and used those for the cards (not detailed content pages) and invited 21 members of the staff to work in teams of three. I used my analysis spreadsheet to store data and analyze it.

The outcome was very interesting. Some cards were grouped in very similar ways—that told me which groups were straightforward. There were a set of cards the teams didn't organize the same—some teams had organized them according to who was responsible and some according to what the noisiest person in the team thought. The remaining cards had been consistently put aside as they didn't fit with anything, which helped me see which topics were outliers.

The team discussions were more useful than the groupings. I learned why some topics were related, how they linked together, what topics staff understood, and what was incomprehensible to everyone. Most importantly, I learned that the company did have a strange set of unrelated responsibilities.

After the card sort, I again analyzed the content and user-research data. I thought about everything I knew and eventually realized I'd never be able to come up with a perfect (or even decent) hierarchical categorization scheme for this client.

In the end, I gave each topic an independent mini-site within the main website. The home page listed all the topics. (They were arranged on the page into rough groupings, but those groupings weren't used anywhere else.) In addition to the topic structure, each team in the company had a page that described what they did and linked to their topics. This was organized according to the company structure.

This approach worked well. The home page clearly showed what the company was involved in, users could jump straight to the topic they were interested in, and managers could see their content listed on the home page and had a page that showed what they were responsible for. Users who knew the company structure (there were many) could find information in that way, too.

CHAPTER 11

Use What You've Learned

Way back at the beginning of the book I talked about the challenge of organizing information in the physical and digital worlds. As I mentioned there, the challenge is not organizing information, but organizing it in a way that works well for other people—the users.

By now I hope I have you convinced that card sorting is a good method for understanding how your users think and for determining potential organization schemes and groupings.

If you have worked through your project and spent time analyzing your card sort data, you should have learned:

- What your users need and how they think.

- Possible organizational schemes for your content.

- Possible top-level categories for your content.

- What content always goes well together.

- What content will be hard to place in any category.

- Whether your audience groups are similar to one another or different.

- And lots more interesting tidbits....

So what do you do with all this interesting stuff? That is going to depend on your project and the reason you ran a card sort in the first place. So I'm going to wrap up with some final tips for really applying what you learned.

Use All Inputs

When you are ready to analyze and use the card sort outcomes, don't forget also to use what you have learned from other user-research activities.

I usually find that there are consistent points that I learn from each method. For example, from interviews I might learn that people are very interested in how much they get paid and what benefits they get, the search logs show a lot of searches for "benefits," and card sort participants created a category called Pay and Benefits. This consistency would make me quite confident in creating a top-level category called Pay and Benefits.

Be Practical

You don't have to use outcomes from the card sort directly. In fact, there may be many times when you deliberately ignore what some or all of the participants provided. If you know that following participants' results would produce an organizational scheme that just wouldn't work, don't do it.

Using the IA Summit example from the previous chapter, I noticed that the Case Studies group had a real mixture of content—some actual case studies and many theoretical presentations. In designing a website for this content, I would not place theoretical presentations into the Case Studies group just because the participants did so—they just aren't case studies. But I will think about why such a grouping occurred (possibly because the titles were ambiguous, or maybe because the Case Studies category was being used in the same way as Other and Miscellaneous sections are used).

For intranet projects, some participants organize the content according to the company structure. If you already know that the company structure doesn't help people find information, then don't use it. Look at the card sort (and your other research) for other ways of organizing your information. I usually spot a set of core topics of interest and use those.

> *Whenever I've worked on intranets, I've found this tension between business units and the overall corporation or organization. The organization often undertakes a redesign, but in reality each business unit operates its section of the intranet as a little fiefdom.*
>
> *I don't think I've ever found a good way to resolve this conflict in card sorting or other research methods. People will take on the organization's point of view during the sort, but then go back to their parochial point of view when they're at their desks.*
>
> —Gene Smith (nform.ca)

Don't Assume

Don't assume anything—think hard about what you have learned from the card sort and its underlying meaning.

During the activity, participants will create groups of cards. But that doesn't mean they necessarily want the website organized like that. All they've done is make some groups. It is up to you to interpret what that means.

A colleague told me a story about a card sort whereby most of the participants created around 20 groups. So the web team dutifully created 20 categories in the site navigation. Then they wondered why everyone complained that it was too many. They had made the mistake of assuming the card sort represented what people actually wanted.

Determine Categories Carefully

In many cases, people use card sorting to create categories, often for website navigation, but also for other uses. It helps to know what you're aiming for when creating categories.

A good set of categories has these characteristics:

- Users understand the categories and can use them to find information and complete tasks.

- The content fits well into the categories, with some, but not too much, overlap.

- The category labels describe the content and match how users think.

You can see that your card-sorting outcomes will help directly with all of these. You learn all about categories that people understand, can use the card sort results to determine where content goes in your categories, and can use the labeling ideas to help you choose labels.

Be Flexible

You don't have to organize a set of content in just one way. Many sets of content can be organized more than one way, and quite sensibly so. For example, events can be organized by time, location, and topic. Don't use the card sort outcomes to find the one true way, but rather to create many ways.

Test Your IA

When you have created a draft set of categories, test them with users to ensure they understand the categories and can use them to find information. I use a method I created a few years ago that I call "card-based classification evaluation" (what a mouthful).[1]

For a card-based classification evaluation, you create two sets of cards. One set lists the draft categories; the other set lists a set of tasks for people to do (such as find out how much travel allowance you are entitled to). You give users a task and ask them what category they would use to find that information. If you have subcategories, you then show the next level and ask users what category they'd choose next. Then you give them another task and repeat the process.

In a very short time, you can find out whether your categories are going to work. If some don't work well, modify them, and test again until they do (see Figure 11.1).

What varieties of wine does this region do best?

When is the harvest festival this year?

1. About the region
2. Our wine
3. Our wineries
4. Eating and drinking
5. What's on

2.1 Key varieties
2.2 Wine show
2.3 Distributors
2.4 Online store

FIGURE 11.1 Card-based classification evaluation helps you test your categories.

---

1 Full details of this approach are at boxesandarrows.com/view/card_based_classification_ evaluation

Don't Rely on a Technique to Do Your Thinking

My final tip encompasses something I've been talking about throughout the entire book.

Remember that you are the one who is doing the thinking, not the technique. You are smart and experienced and allowed to have good ideas—card sorting (and other techniques) is an aid to provide insights and help you create great solutions. But you are the one who puts it all together into a great solution. Follow your instincts, take some risks, and try new approaches.

APPENDIX

Documentation

C ard sorting is one input into the bigger picture of user research for a project. As such, documentation is not strictly necessary—you can use the insights you gained without having to write them down.

But even when I don't *need* to document the card sort, I still make sure I do it. Why? Because documentation has many benefits:

- When you have to explain something in writing, you are forced to justify your findings. I often start writing and discover that some of my conclusions aren't supported by the data.

- Documenting the outcome gives legitimacy to the process. It shows that you thought about what you were doing and what came out of the activity.

- It helps share what you learned, and may allow others to represent the findings on your behalf.

- It provides additional transparency for your decisions—if someone later questions a recommendation, you can show where the idea came from.

As with any documentation process, the first step is to decide whom you are trying to communicate with and what you need to tell them. This will help you make sure that your report is as effective as possible.

The amount of detail you include in your documentation depends on many factors, including the situation you are working in, the amount of time you have, and the complexity of the project. If you are working closely with colleagues in a team, you may need to produce only a bare-bones report that acts as a wrap-up of the card sort. But if you are working as a consultant, you will almost certainly want to produce a detailed, polished report.

I have outlined three different levels of documentation, from bare bones to very detailed[1], and some tips for all types of reports.

---

1 I borrowed this three-layer approach from Dan Brown's *Communicating Design: Developing Website Documentation for Design and Planning.* New Riders, 2006.

Bare-Bones Report

As the least detailed level of documentation, a bare-bones report should provide basic documentation about the card sort—enough for someone to understand what you did and what you learned, and should be sufficient for you (or someone else) to refer back to in the future. A bare-bones report also is a good way to make sure that your results are available quickly, perhaps while you work on a more detailed report.

As a basic record of what occurred, this level of documentation may not include any in-depth analysis. Readers of this type of report may need to do much of the interpretation themselves.

A bare-bones report should include the following information:

- Background about card sorting and what it can help you learn.

- Why you decided to run a card sort, and what you hoped to achieve.

- How many participants were involved and how you recruited them.

- How you ran the card sort.

- A table of summary data from the card sort.

- A summary of findings highlighting consistencies and inconsistencies.

- Key insights that you want to draw attention to.

- A reference to the full results for people to explore.

Detailed Report

This second level of documentation is fairly detailed. The aim of this type of report is to go further in explaining your analysis and implications.

This type of document should include everything that is in the bare-bones report. But it should go beyond that and provide an interpretation of the results. This report could also include:

- A summary of the key issues you identified and any recommendations.

- A list of groups created by participants, with the most common cards for each group.

- A list of different ways people described similar concepts.

- An analysis of the issues you identified with interpretation about why they may have occurred.

- A detailed list of recommendations, with data to back up those decisions.

Comprehensive Report

The third level of documentation adds a layer of polish to the detailed report and aims to situate the activity in a broader context. This report can also include:

- Information from other activities that supports or contradicts what you learned in the card sort.

- A deeper analysis of qualitative data from the card sort.

- Information about how the card sort outcomes will be or have been used within the project.

An example report for all three types is available on the book's website at ᴙ www.rosenfeldmedia.com.

Index

ACKNOWLEDGMENTS

Everyone says it, but it is actually true: While this book is mostly my effort, it has been hugely improved via help from many other people.

First, a general thanks to everyone who read chapters and provided great comments: Steve Baty, Dan Brown, Dustin Chambers, Ruth Ellison, Leo Frishberg, Patrick Kennedy, Jorge Larango, Sam Ng, Kristi Olsen, Gene Smith, Peter Van Dijck, Steven Weintraub, and Alex Wright.

I also want to say a special thank you to two particularly special reviewers. Leo Frishberg and Dan Willis both did something quite hard and told me how bad my early version was. And Dan rewrote my entire chapter structure into something that made sense. Thanks so much to both of you for being brave, honest, and constructive—your comments made a huge difference, and this book is much better because of it.

It was great to be able to involve my closest friends as well. Ruth Ellison took photos and Caronne Carruthers-Taylor, Nigel Carruthers-Taylor, and Andrew Boyd posed for them. Thanks for sharing your time and company to help me illustrate how card sorting works.

One of the things I really like about this book is the case studies and quotes. They show that I'm not the only person who thinks this way, and they help highlight the key points. Thank you to everyone who provided case studies and allowed me to print their words.

I also want to thank everyone who has participated in a card sort I've run, including everyone who has done the winery card sort as part of one of my information architecture workshops. You've all helped me learn how people think, and I design better products as a result.

And the last thank you is to all the nice folks who have used my analysis spreadsheet and then told me how good it is. It is rewarding to see that something I knocked together for myself was actually handy for you. One day I'll hook up with a smart programmer and make a better tool to do this.

ABOUT THE AUTHOR

Donna Spencer is a freelance information architect, interaction designer, and writer. That means she is responsible for what you see on the computer screen—website navigation, applications, forms, categories, and words.

She works mostly on large, messy projects like government websites and intranets, internal business applications, and web applications. But sometimes she gets to work on funky, small projects and likes them just as much. Some of her projects take months to do, and sometimes she works with agile programming teams to do small amounts of work in short bursts.

One of the most important parts of her work is to get a good understanding of the needs of the users and make sure the system she's working on is as usable as possible. Given that she's quite fond of people, she loves doing user research and running usability tests to understand the people she's designing for. She also sketches screens, draws wireframes, and makes prototypes.

But Donna likes something even more than designing usable systems. She loves teaching. She's a very experienced speaker and regularly teaches workshops at conferences and in-house. She also presents at local and international conferences on the topics of information architecture, interaction design, the Web, writing, and more.

When she's not doing client work or teaching, Donna is running a conference (UX Australia), preparing new workshops, thinking about what book to write next, and trying to get through the big pile of books on her floor.

CPSIA information can be obtained
at www.ICGtesting.com
Printed in the USA
JSHW011456020723
44043JS00001B/3